What's The Matter With The US Economy?

Peter Gutmann

authorHOUSE®

AuthorHouse™
1663 Liberty Drive, Suite 200
Bloomington, IN 47403
www.authorhouse.com
Phone: 1-800-839-8640

First published by AuthorHouse 10/15/2007

ISBN: 978-1-4343-4373-4 (sc)

Library of Congress Control Number: 2007907755

Printed in the United States of America
Bloomington, Indiana

This book is printed on acid-free paper.

PREFACE TO
WHAT'S THE MATTER WITH THE US ECONOMY?

The US economy does many things right. But it also does many things wrong. This book is focused on those aspects of the US economy that require some correction, in the hope that corrective action will eventually be forthcoming.

It is not intended to cover every economic problem area, but rather to focus on some of the most salient ones.

The book is divided into 26 chapters in 8 sections. The reader will recognize that there is an inevitable overlap between some of the topics covered. After all, it is but one economy. I have tried to keep such overlap to a minimum.

This book is addressed to the intelligent general reader. It does not use equations, graphs, diagrams, footnotes or arcane gobbledygook.

New York
October 2007

TABLE OF CONTENTS

INTRODUCTION

Here are the themes covered.

Globalization: The huge increase in the world labor force engaged in trade, the revolution in inexpensive communications, the rapid industrialization of a number of Asian countries, the shifts in comparative advantage between countries, the rising international competition in more and more labor categories, the great trade imbalances, as well as the effects of the increase in the price of internationally traded petroleum, all have become major issues that the US has not handled particularly well.

Social Justice: There has been rising focus on the facts of income inequality in the US; on the tripartite division between the poor, the middle class and the rich as this has become more poignant; on the ever growing, ever more pressing and ever more expensive entitlements. Congress exercises a great deal of influence over these issues. So the question arises: whom does Congress represent most, the multi hundred million consumers or the much smaller number of producers?

Life's Essentials: These include health, education, housing, work and retirement, as well as the use of energy. This whole huge area is replete with problems.

Personal Risk: There is also an underlying lifetime issue: risk. Who bears the risk? Does most of the US public want to bear more risk or less risk in their lives?

Macroeconomic Issues: Will there be enough demand to assure high levels of national output? Should and will household savings increase? Should and will the Federal deficit decrease? Can we continue to live beyond our means? Are we mortgaging the future? How does income distribution affect all this? What does the remortgaging of houses for consumption purposes do to savings and retirement income?

The State - Federal, State and Local: Who gets the tax dollars? How large should these be? Are governments overcommitted? Who is to be taxed? How are expenditures directed?

The World of Assets: More and more assets of every kind have become more and more liquid over recent decades. Sooner ar later, just about every asset, short of human beings, will be turned into something readily convertible into cash. What has this liquidity sloshing around the world done to the economy? What were its limits? What is the impact of slicing asset pools into different risk classes?

Finally, there are a number of other matters. There is the important subject of international labor movements, i.e. immigration. What kind should we have? There is the subject of waste. There is the subject of excess. And there are others as well.

PART 1: INTERNATIONAL: GLOBALIZATION

Chapter 1

THE DOLLAR AS A PONZI SCHEME

In a Ponzi scheme, named after Charles Ponzi who conducted such a fraud in the early 1920's, early investors in an investment scheme are paid back their capital as well as promised interest or profits from the influx of funds of later investors. The scheme collapses when the influx of funds from later investors becomes insufficient to do so.

At present, the US has a huge, unsustainable import surplus totaling around six per cent of GDP. This is financed through enormous US borrowing from foreigners and sale of US assets to them. In recent years the private sector capital inflows have not been sufficient to finance this import surplus. So, foreign central banks, particularly some Asian central banks and some Middle Eastern oil producing countries' central banks have taken up the slack.

As a result. these central banks acquired huge amounts of US treasury bills, notes and bonds as well as US "Agencies" and some other US assets. The motives of many of these countries were clear. By selling their own currencies and buying the dollars needed to acquire US assets, they kept down the value of their own currencies and kept up the value of the dollar, so that their exports would remain cheap.

Recently, this is beginning to be supplemented by new sovereign wealth funds where foreign governments and their agencies sell their own currencies, buy dollars and then purchase stocks, businesses or parts of businesses in the US. Of course this adds an element of risk above and beyond the exchange rate risk for those countries. These types of investment also serve to keep down the value of their own currencies.

What is wrong with these purchases of dollars? Well, there has to be a continuing influx of dollar purchases by later international investors to permit the earlier international investors to take their capital out of the US again at their initially expected value of the dollar. If the later investors (to a large extent the foreign central banks) decide to reduce their purchases of dollars, the value of the dollar will fall. Then the earlier international investors will take a a loss.

What happens if an earlier international investor decides to sell a large amount of US Treasuries and take the proceeds out of the US?

There are two aspects to this. First, there will be a domestic US effect. Interest rates will go up and prices of Treasuries will go down as the market for Treasuries adjusts. Second, as the supply of dollars internationally, i.e. the demand for foreign currencies, increases, the value of the dollar in terms of foreign currencies drops, perhaps substantially, depending on the size of the transaction. The early investor in Treasuries will take a loss.

So, somewhat similar to a Ponzi scheme, the earlier international investors in Treasuries via the dollar are dependent on a continuing influx of later investors in US Treasuries via the dollar.

Realistically could, say, the Chinese central bank liquidate a large portion of its multi hundred billion US Treasuries securities portfolio and bring the proceeds back to Chinese currency? The answer is, "no". They are stuck. They are stuck with this investment, which is an investment in an overvalued currency, namely the dollar, that is bound to decline relative to their own currency in the future. The people of China will bear the loss. This matter has not escaped the Chinese authorities.

So, what is wrong with the American economy? After all, the eventual loss for the people of China when the value of the dollar declines is a gain for the people of America.

But, in the meantime, the costs to the American economy of an overvalued dollar are the costs of a loss in competitiveness. This is the current situation and it is serious. An overvalued dollar makes exports too expensive and imports too cheap. It increases the shift of US industries out of the country. Industries involved in exports are hurt and so are industries competing with imports. Of course the very decline in the value of the dollar that we have already experienced so far has tended to increase exports, decrease imports and reduce the import surplus somewhat. But the import surplus still remains huge, since exports are far less than imports. It will remain huge.

How long can this system of ever "new" investors in US Treasuries via the dollar go on? Only as long as foreign central banks are willing to buy massive amounts of dollars at exchange rates not very dissimilar to those reigning today. When they eventually decide to cut back, i.e. buy only at lower dollar values, the value of the dollar will drop.

Seen as a Ponzi scheme, this system does appear somewhat peculiar? Why? Because the early investors and the later investors in dollars are, to a substantial degree, the same. This means that such investors walk into this system with eyes wide open. They knowingly enter such a Ponzi scheme and the inevitable capital losses that it entails in the future.

3

Why do they do it? The investors, the central banks such as the central bank of China, do so because the gain in competitiveness for their nations. They are willing to bear the large future capital losses in order to benefit from their even larger gains in competitiveness in the meantime. Their overwhelming priority is economic development right now. It is a tradeoff between present competitiveness and future capital loss. .

Chapter 2

THE LAW OF ONE PRICE

The law of one price is a famous law in economics. It states that identical tradable goods, subject to transportation costs, sell at the same price everywhere, as long as there are no impediments to trade such as tariffs or quotas. Of course, in the real world, there are plenty of impediments, so all tradable goods do not sell at identical prices everywhere.

This law also applies to tradable services. But the vast majority of services are not traded internationally. Haircuts are not tradable, except in the close vicinity of an open international border. But some services are tradable, for example certain kinds of insurance services. And more services are becoming tradable continuously.

Labor costs do not obey the law of one price since there is no free flow of labor internationally, indeed far from it. Immigration restrictions exist just about everywhere. The many impediments to the free flow of labor are not going to go away. Of course there are legal flows of labor as well as the illegal flows, from poor to rich countries which do have a very limited effect on reducing wage differences between different countries. But large differences exist and will continue to exist.

However, there are indirect effects that also tend to reduce wage differentials between rich and poor countries. As goods production moves from rich to poor countries, this tends to increase wages in the poor countries and reduce them in the rich countries. This effect operates on those wage categories that are most involved in such international shifts in production.

Historically, these categories have largely been unskilled and semiskilled workers. Industries such as textiles and electronic assembly operations have moved to a very large extent from rich to poor countries. In textiles this includes spinning, weaving and apparel. Cheaper labor in specific categories is the principal reason. This has been the case even though productivity of seemingly identical labor in poor countries is less than in rich countries. One way of putting this is to say that poor countries have a comparative advantage in textile production and electronic assembly.

But, with the relentless advance of technology, comparative advantage shifts. Usually, this shift is from rich countries to poor countries. But it may also go the other way, particularly if the industry becomes highly automated, so that labor costs become far less significant.

The shift in comparative advantage is not only due to rising skill levels in poor countries, but also due to technological changes such as the enormous drop in the costs of international communications which has put more and more services into play. This has affected areas such as call centers (mostly for English speaking countries), advice in running PC's, Macs and all kinds of software, printers and so forth, as well as a variety of commercial "outsourcing" of certain computer software functions. Some are quite novel, such as work in the US during the day and in India during our night, speeding up the process of creating new software.

The shifts in comparative advantage are at a greater pace than ever before. This means that adaptation to these changes must also be at a greater pace than ever before. As international competition moves up the labor skill ladder, the displaced workers in the rich countries must shift to other employment and other occupations.

Labor market flexibility becomes ever more important. And the focus on education has to become more and more significant. Education and reeducation, particularly job related education on a lifetime basis, becomes more critical. In the US many community colleges are taking up this task. But their success depends partly on the preexisting general educational level of the students. In far too many cases this is woefully inadequate due to failures at the elementary and high school levels, and even the college level. This failure is greatest in mathematics, science and technology. In fact it is so bad that the US is far from self sufficient in engineers. Large numbers must be imported from other countries, including some of the poorer countries.

Essentially, the rich countries must be increasingly nimble in their educational and labor markets. And they must realize that unskilled middle class jobs are disappearing. both because of rapid automation with faster technological change and because of the increased international competition up the labor skill ladder.

PART 2: SOCIAL JUSTICE

Chapter 3

ACCESS

Access is very important in the economy. Access to the right places can serve to increase income, procure better jobs, progress faster in the work environment, live in better neighborhoods, enter into different social groups, obtain more desirable legislation, alter the tax laws in favor of specific groups, and much more.

There has been a substantial amount of progress in the last few decades in reducing impediments to access in a number of areas, particularly in regard to discrimination in jobs and housing as well as primary and secondary schooling plus higher education. However, much remains to be done.

Access tends to involve money. Yes, it turns out that access usually requires money, but not only money. In turn, better access yields a monetary return.

Access to education builds human capital, and human capital has a substantial rate of return. But at the primary and, to a lesser extent, secondary level, the financing of schools is typically heavily dependent on the local tax base. This limits access to good education. Where the area is poor, the tax base is low, the schools poor and the educational quality mediocre. This limits access to higher education. In addition, higher education is expensive. This too limits access, particularly when funding of students in terms of direct financial aid and loans declines.

Clearly needed is a more level playing field that can only be obtained with shift in the funding of primary and secondary schools away from its dependence on the local tax base, plus further shifts in the funding of higher education.

Access to better jobs requires access to better education. In our complicated world there is really no substitute.

Access to faster progress in the work environment requires willingness to promote based on merit, not the personal predilections of employers. This means access without discrimination. It also increasingly requires a continuous effort of lifetime learning on the part of the employee, not to mention just plain hard work.

Access to better neighborhoods with better housing and schools usually requires higher income. But the better jobs with the higher income are largely based on better education. In turn, the better education is available in the better neighborhoods where schools are financed by a higher tax base. This sequence of neighborhoods - schools -jobs - neighborhoods - schools has come full circle. It will remain so as long as the largely local system of school financing remains.

There are still other considerations. The better teachers tend to gravitate to the better school systems, not only due to better prospects but also due to better conditions. This is particularly important in large city systems with a single tax base but with widely varying quality in their schools.

We now come to a somewhat different type of access, the access that is so influential in legislation, the tax system, income distribution and other facets of our society.

On the national level, this comes back to a fundamental question, "whom does Congress represent - consumers or producers?" The answer, of course, is that it is a mixture. Congress people and Senators need money, lots of money. Elections are expensive, very expensive. And perks, such as free lunches, have been attractive to Congress and its top staff people. In addition some in Congress need more personal funds to supplement their salaries, whether legal or illegal. But under public pressure, Congress has now passed legislation to eliminate a number of perks.

Elections are financed by political contributions. Those who contribute the most funds tend to have the greatest political clout. In addition, they have the funds needed to hire the major part of the army of lobbyists circling in Washington.

There are two kinds of political contributions - those from political supporters and those from contributors who want to buy access. The latter are legion. They are very important to politicians who almost inevitably have large election connected expenditures.

The country has to face a very fundamental issue. As long as politicians are required to finance their political campaigns, they will find ways of raising the funds, regardless of restrictions imposed by election laws. Ways are found around these. Indeed ways must be found. The only current alternative is to leave the field largely to the very wealthy who can self finance. That is hardly desirable.

What can be done? The system can be made much more transparent, in the hope that transparency will give voters the information required to hold their legislators more accountable. But it would be idle to expect that the impact of producers, as opposed to consumers, will decline drastically. They will still buy access.

Right now, for example, lobbyists "bundle" a substantial number of political contributions and present these at one time to legislators in order to gain access. Is this going to vanish with transparency? No.

What does this system do? It produces legislation favorable to lots of special interests. It heavily impacts the tax system. Different types of income pay different tax rates. In particular, the types of income found among the top income groups often pay lesser tax rates. And there are numerous special provisions in the tax code that have been openly passed in the past or slipped into legislation in the dead of night at the behest of lobbyists, provisions that favor not only specific business interests but also the higher income groups. So, we have a tax code riddled with exceptions and exemptions, a tax code often called a "disgrace".

So, access counts. It is expensive, but it produces results. It fundamentally alters the democratic process. It certainly benefited special interests of all sorts. On a national basis, it alters the after-tax income distribution. It also alters the "perceived fairness" of the process. It rewards those with the funds to buy access. But it is an entrenched system, exceedingly hard to change, as long as the whole electoral system floats on money.

Chapter 4

ENTITLEMENTS

An entitlement is an unrequited payment or service received by anyone who meets the requirements for that particular entitlement. For example, anyone in the US who has reached 65 years of age and meets the requirements for basic Medicare (hospitalization) is entitled to receive such hospital care as defined.

Entitlements have been growing as a proportion of the Federal budget for decades and now make up not far from half the Federal budget. They have also been growing as a proportion of the State budgets This is not only true of the US, but also of other highly developed, industrialized countries and even in developing nations.

By far the biggest share of entitlements in the US is part of the so-called safety net. This is true of the three largest, Social Security, Medicare and Medicaid. But there are other entitlements such as the farm subsidies that are different in character.

Entitlements have become an ever larger proportion of the GDP. As the cost of these programs rises, the financing must also rise. This means that one or more of three possibilities will have to be chosen in the future: (a) a larger proportion of the tax dollar may have to be devoted to these programs at the expense of competing government programs; (b) the amount of tax dollars collected by the government plus the deficit, as a proportion of GDP, may have to increase; (c) the programs may have to be cut.

Social Security and Medicare are extremely popular and Medicaid is extremely necessary. So, the size and rapid growth of these programs will probably require tax increases. In some cases, specific taxes have already begun to rise. This is the case for Medicare B, the part of Medicare that pays for physician services. It has also been true in the past for Social Security. But much more is needed. For Social Security this can fairly readily be achieved, at least in principle if not in practical politics, through a combination of higher Social Security (FICA) tax and a rise in the existing income cutoff point for Social Security tax payments, combined with a revision in Social Security benefit payments to the higher income groups.

However, for Medicare, it is far, far more difficult due to the size, growth rate and open-endedness of future payment magnitudes. Probably a combination of tax increases, deductibles, co-payments and, eventually, rationing of medical treatment will emerge. The same process of aging of the population plus increases in medical technology affects Medicaid costs. And here the States are heavily involved as well as the Federal Government.

Entitlements also involve some income redistribution, both on the payment side and on the expenditure side. For both Social Security and Medicare, there is an intergenerational compact. On the payment side, those working now make the payments. On the expenditure side, those over 65 (for Social Security many over 62), most of whom are retired, secure the benefits. The implicit promise to those working now is that the following generations will make the same arrangements when the present workforce reaches retirement age. That is likely to become a problem since the retirement population, relative to the total population, will be rising in future years.

In addition, within the Social Security system, there is some income redistribution, i.e. there is no exact actuarial relationship between payments and the later receipts after retirement. In Medicare, this is more obvious since payments vary by income while medical services, at least in principle, do not; in addition, ever since the income cap on the Medicare tax was removed, this difference in payments has become even greater. Also about three quarters of Medicare B (for doctors) is paid through the general Federal tax system. These payment differences will be further augmented as of 2007 through still higher payments, for those with higher income, for Medicare B. Finally, as in all insurance programs, there is a transfer from the healthy to the sick.

For the Medicaid program for the poor, there is no intergenerational compact. This is an income redistribution through the general tax systems of both Federal and State.

All of these entitlement programs have to be supplemented by private funds. Governments simply cannot afford to cover full costs, especially when the size and growth rates of the programs are contemplated. Medicare already requires supplemental insurance programs privately paid to cover actual costs. So does Social Security which is really insufficient to pay for full retirement. Medicaid, in truth, also requires additional funds, although such funds are usually not available to the low income public using Medicaid. Serious health problems are all too often not covered or inadequately covered. This remains an unresolved issue.

The Social Security and Medicare entitlements are very popular, very large and have great political support. They are obviously supported by those who receive the funds and services. Medicare is also supported by those who deliver the services. There is tremendous pressure, particularly for Medicare, to make it larger in size, covering more extensive services and become more attractive to participants. This is not true of the Medicaid program as viewed by the general public, who regard it as an expensive, if necessary, stepchild with too many participants and too much fraud. Its political support is limited.

Americans, by and large, do not want to bear health risks. This has become obvious in the political sphere. In fact they pushed mightily for expansion of government health programs into the drug area, adding a new expense for government, an expense that will grow. Health insurance, widely available, is playing a more and more important part in elections at both the Federal and the State levels,

And, as the baby boomers edge closer to retirement, Social Security, as well as health, will continue to receive increasing attention. The failure of the Bush Administration in its attempt to change Social Security in a fundamental way, a way that increased risk, is indicative of the popularity of the existing program. It is also indicative of the unwillingness of voters to support changes that would have resulted in more risk.

Chapter 5

THREE SOCIETIES: SEPARATE AND UNEQUAL

Income differences basically have divided the US into three groups: the poor, the middle class and the wealthy. These differ in a number of salient respects.

The poor are roughly the lowest 40 per cent of income tax filers. This figure corresponds approximately to the 36 per cent of the public that has either no bank account or uses a bank account only rarely. This group had an annual income of about $25,850 or less (for 2001 at 2005 prices.) The poor received some 9 per cent of US income. Within this group is a subgroup, essentially those who are in poverty, with an annual income of $13,475 or less.

The middle class comprised the next 55 per cent of income tax filers, those with annual income between about $25,850 and $162,350. The middle class received about 58 per cent of US income.

Peter Gutmann

The rich comprised the top 5 per cent of the population, those receiving more than $162,350 per year, about 33 per cent of US income (all figures subject to rounding).

The top 10 per cent, i.e. the rich plus the upper middle class, got more of US income than the bottom 80 per cent.

These three groups, to a very large extent, live different lives, in different communities, have different jobs and live in a different social milieu. Outside the workplace, there is very limited social communication between the groups. Even within the workplace, there isn't a great deal of communication at the same level.

The degree of home ownership is lowest among the poor and highest among the rich. And the rich, and to some extent the upper range of the middle class, increasingly live in different gated communities. The poor are far more likely to be renters than owners.

The three groups to a large extent live in geographically separate communities with different school systems. Those of the rich, and to an extent those of the middle class, are much better funded than those of the poor. As a result, the quality of the school systems also varies. And the children of the rich are far more likely to attend private school than those of the other groups.

The three groups also have different access to medical care. For the rich, only the best - and most expensive - will do. At the other end, the poor simply have to make do - with whatever is available. They line up for Medicaid or go to emergency rooms. The rich are unlikely to worry much about possible expensive emergencies and procedures. The middle class worries a lot, due to lack of adequate insurance, no insurance at all and insurance tied to an uncertain job. They worry about dropping out of the middle class altogether as well as potential bankruptcy Most of the poor qualify for Medicaid. They also worry a lot since it is all too frequent for the working poor to drop into actual poverty.

The rich spend very little time worrying about retirement since it is usually well funded. The top 5 per cent in the US own some 60 per cent of US assets. The middle class worries a lot since they typically have not set aside enough funds to take care of their retirement. The poor are stuck with with only the inadequate Social Security payments or depend completely on family contributions.

On the subject of voting behavior, the poor participate far less. As a result, their political influence is very low. The middle class and the rich have far greater voting participation. But only the rich have the funds to make major contributions to candidates and receive major political influence through access. So, the poor are under represented and the rich over represented in practical politics.

Then, the poor are far more likely to be Black or Hispanic than the middle class and the rich. Such ethnic differences simply magnify the difference between the poor and the other two groups.

All of these differences impact social attitudes. In Europe, the general attitude is that the poor were dealt a bad hand of cards in life's selections. As a result, they should get a helping hand. In the US the attitude is much more likely to be that the poor have only themselves to blame and are little deserving.

The poor can only dream the American dream. They are unlikely to rise very far in the economic struggle. They have to live with their dreams, unfulfilled by a harsh reality. The middle class also dreams the American dream, but with much more of a chance to convert that dream to reality. For many, hope springs eternal. In fact, for much of the middle class, their behavior apes that of the rich they would like to become rather than that of the middle class they are. These aspirations become a type of reality.

This separation into these three groups raises a serious question. Is it healthy? To what extent does it become a problem, perhaps a serious one? It turns out that it depends in part on the degree to which long term rising living standards due to long term productivity advances are widely shared. If they are spread across all groups, dissatisfaction with the existing degree of separation, both economic and social, is likely to be contained. If long term productivity gains are largely appropriated by the upper income groups, dissatisfaction will rise, with all the resulting political and social consequences that entails.

Unfortunately, in recent decades, the economic differences between the rich and the other two groups have been magnified, with the rich appropriating a substantially larger share of the total. The result has been increasing attention focused on income distribution, an attention that is likely to increase in the future. This is particularly true because Federal taxation policy in recent years has only exacerbated these economic differences between the rich and the other two groups.

Other democracies also have substantial income differentials between the groups, but not as much as in the US. The degree of the differential is unhealthy. And the distribution of the productivity gains in the past couple of decades is unhealthy. It has become a problem. And it is a problem that will come more to the fore in future US Administrations and Congresses when tax policy is debated.

Chapter 6

THE RICH, THE POOR AND THE MIDDLE CLASS: WHO GETS WHAT?

The US has one of the most unequal income distributions in the world. It is so unequal that it raises questions about democracy in an electoral system powered by money.

Compared to the countries of Western Europe, the top tenth of US households receives about 10 percentage points more of the national income, and everyone else that much less. This is a gigantic difference.

On top of that, taxes on the wealthy have been reduced in recent years while taxes on the middle class are increasing as the notorious Alternative Minimum Tax moves further downward into middle class incomes.

Wealth has largely captured the Bush Administration, as shown by its income tax policy and by repeated attempts to repeal the Estate Tax, now renamed the death tax, a tax that hits the larger estates left by the death of their owners.

Finally, the fruits of US productivity increases have been very unequally distributed in recent decades, A very large share has gone to the upper income groups, particularly the top fraction of one per cent, leaving large sections of the middle class with relatively little increase.

The middle class is under pressure, as there is expansion at the low and high income ends. This is an important matter, since the stability of democracies is tied to a substantial middle class, without very large extremes of wealth and poverty.

The basic data on income distribution, derived from Internal Revenue figures, was given in the last chapter.

So, what is the relationship between incomes among the poor, the middle class and the rich?

The average middle class tax filer made about 4.8 times the income of the average poor tax filer. The average rich tax filer had an income 29.4 times that of the average poor filer. And the average super rich (the top one out of a thousand, making more than $1,589,696) had an income 359.6 times that of the average poor filer.

The differences between the middle class and the rich are also very high. The average rich tax filer had an income 12.2 times that of the average middle class filer. The average super rich tax filer had an income 74.8 times that of the average middle class filer.

In addition, there are considerable differences within the poor, within the middle class and within the rich.

The average top half of the poor made 2.6 times the average income of the bottom half of the poor.

The top 5 percentage points of the middle class, i.e. the upper middle class (out of the 55 percentage points total, making between $117,001 and $162,352) had an average income 3.8 times that of the bottom 20 percentage points in the middle class.

Finally, the average super rich had an income 21.3 times that of the merely rich (the 95th to 99th percentile of the population, making between $162,351 and $387,507).

Next, we come to the subject of changes in income distribution over a substantial period of time. The recent Becker-Gordon study sheds light on the historical trend. It deals with median wage and salary income changes from 1966 to 2001. The median is the middle number of a series of numbers.

Between 1966 and 2001, a period of 35 years, real median wage and salary income, adjusted for inflation, rose some 11 per cent. This was the rise at the middle of the income distribution.

Income at the 90th percentile rose 58 per cent during these 35 years. Income at the 99th percentile rose 121 per cent. The rise was 236 per cent at the 99.9th percentile. And at the 99.99th percentile, with 13,000 of the highest paid income earners above that figure, the rise was 617 per cent.

Obviously, there was a dramatic shift in income distribution for wages and salaries towards the very highest income earners, This tiny proportion of US income recipients took a huge share of the productivity increase during this third of a century. For the period 1966 to 2001 only 10 per cent of America's workers had an increase in income at least as rapid as the US productivity growth rate.

There are two groups in particular that gained hugely. One group is largely composed of sports figures, Hollywood stars, TV personalities and other media stars. These benefited through greater exposure in TV, movies and other media on a worldwide basis. In the case of sports, rule changes were fundamental.

The other group appears to be largely made up of chief executives of substantial companies plus financial entrepreneurs. The huge increase in the financial remuneration of CEO's, even when performance was poor, seems to indicate a failure in corporate governance. Many CEO'S in effect increased their own incomes at the expense of potential corporate profits. Boards of directors stood by, collected their own benefits, and failed to do their job of supervising management.

In summary, the rich have a very large share of the national product in the US, far more than in Western Europe And, over the last four decades this large share has become even larger. In addition, the top income groups have benefited from substantial tax reductions.

From a public policy point of view, as Becker and Gordon note, when more tax money is needed by the Federal Government, it need not look very far.

We can misquote the famous bank robber Willie Sutton somewhat, "you turn to the rich 'because that's where the money is'". After all, the upper 5 per cent take nearly one-third of US income, have average incomes 12.2 times that of the middle class, and 29.4 times that of the poor.

The poor are in no position to pay much of anything. So, whatever is not paid by the middle class will have to be paid by the rich.

Chapter 7

WHOM DOES CONGRESS REPRESENT: CONSUMERS OR PRODUCERS?

Congress makes the laws, with a heavy input from the White House. The 100 Senators from the 50 States and the 435 members of the House of Representatives elected in an equal number of Congressional districts are the lawmakers.

Lawmakers are, of course, elected by registered voters. At least in theory they represent the interests of the electorate. Needless to say, these interest are not unitary. Inevitably there are always many competing interests,

Voters are also consumers and most come from the middle class. Just about all have economic interests. They need income to pay their bills for food, housing, education, travel, taxes and all the rest. In addition, they also have non-economic interests of various kinds.

Senators and Congressmen and women also have to pay their bills. But they have special and very heavy bills, namely bills for the increasingly large expenditures required to run for office. Who pays these bills?

The answer is that contributors pay the bills. But who are these contributors? The bigger contributors who pay most of the bills are those who have something to gain from the future expected votes and have gained from the actual past votes of the lawmaker who receives the contribution. They also anticipate that their contribution plus those of like-minded other contributors will influence the voting behavior of the lawmaker.

The bigger contributors tend to be those who have business interests. Most of them are high income, wealthy and special interest. And there are the lobbyists, thousands of them, who inundate Washington, representing mostly narrow special interests. The lobbyists and the political operators arrange to channel substantial political contributions to the Congress people and Senators where these political contributions are expected to do the most good for their clients. There are exceptions of course; some wealthy contributors actually have in mind the common weal.

So, most Washington legislators have to pay close attention to the interests of their contributors if they expect to finance the next election. They spend a large amount of time on the phone soliciting contributions and on fund raising affairs. Failure to do this effectively risks electoral defeat at the hands of an opponent who is better financed.

The interests that largely fund these political electoral contests are mostly producer interests. To a high degree they are business interests and the interests of the upper income groups. They are quite different from the economic interests of the general public and quite different from the economic interests of the middle class.

All this means that Washington legislators represent producers at least as much as consumers. This has profound implications for tax policy, regulations, business subsidies, government contracts and a host of other issues.

This is not to say that producer interests trump every consumer interest. Far from it. There are issues where there is intense national voter interest, such as immigration reform and Social Security matters. Business alone cannot prevail in those types of issues. But there are many matters, particularly arcane tax and regulatory legislation, that are very important to some sectors of business and do have economic implications for the general public, and yet the public hardly knows what is going on. On these, producer interests will prevail. In their totality, such issues are big and have a large economic impact.

There have been many attempts, a number of laws and a host of rhetoric devoted to contend with political financing. But the fundamental problem remains. That problem is the large amount of money needed to run successfully for office. Vast amounts are needed to pay for TV presentations and air time. Indeed, due to the costs involved as well as time spent in fund raising, the sprinkling of multimillionaires found among successful politicians has grown larger, since they can and do pay much of their own bills. They don't have to go through as much of the eternal required fund raising.

The US political system, not by chance, floats on money. This changes everything. The whole governmental system is shifted more and more away from consumer interests to producer interests, as well as the interests of the wealthy. This is well known of course. It is exactly this shift that makes meaningful reform so very difficult, since the groups able to spend large amounts of money are most unlikely to give up a system that has been so very successful in protecting their interests.

The sea of money has also been used in shifting votes of the public. At election times in particular, a number of "social issues" are trundled out to wean voters away from their economic interests. These issues include flag burning, single sex marriage, adoption of English as the official language, etc. Such issues directly affect very few in the general voting public. In contrast, economic issues affect practically everyone. Wide publicity, numerous TV ads, friendly talk show campaigns, all are used at considerable cost to shift voter attention away from economic issues that do affect them directly in favor of some of the social issues that do not.

The basic conclusion is that "money talks". It certainly can swing elections. Result: producer issues gain in Congress; consumer issues decline.

PART 3: LIFE'S ESSENTIALS

Chapter 8

HEALTH

The American medical system at its best is the best in the world. But it has serious problems - cost, access, insurance, efficiency, high annual expenditure rates of increase, public anxiety. These put it well down in international comparisons of public satisfaction with different medical systems.

The US spends more on medical outlays, now some 16 plus per cent of the GDP and rapidly growing, than any other country in the world, in some cases nearly double the proportion of the GDP spent by other high income countries. The medical field has become the great job creation vehicle of the US economy. The Sunday New York Times, for example, can have page after page of advertisements of jobs in the health field.

It is obvious, of course,that we cannot all be employed in the health industry. The rapid growth of health expenditures, eating up ever higher proportions of the GDP, fueled by rapid advances in expensive new technology, the quick application of that technology in medicine, and the aging of the population, will have to come to an end sooner or later. This means that there will be more and more just plain rationing of health care in future years.

Peter Gutmann

The whole subject of health is one that creates considerable anxiety among the American public. It is not simply that not far from 50 million are uninsured. A great many who do have some insurance are not adequately insured for a major health problem.

In addition, more and more must directly pay a larger and larger percentage of their insurance premium. And with deductibles, coinsurance, limitations and exclusions, the health bill mounts even for those reasonably well insured. The result is that an increasing number either cannot afford insurance at all or can only afford inadequate insurance.

Considering that the lowest 40 per cent of US income tax filers only receive some 9 per cent of total US income, there are a great many people involved. And in the middle class, the next 55 per cent of income tax filers, there are a large number who cannot afford insurance that is adequate.

There are even more who are fearful of job loss with the accompanying loss of health insurance as well as income. This only exacerbates their continuing anxiety about payment of medical expenses.

These anxieties will never go away until there is some sort of system, almost surely a combination of public and private, that provides everyone the assurance of adequate medical care for a lifetime, regardless of job status or state of health. Even then, some anxieties will remain since such comprehensive systems as they exist in other countries leave much to be desired. In most of these countries, the middle class and above buys additional private health insurance.

Any system that provides adequate health care to everyone is bound to involve subsidies and some income redistribution. This is clear since many will never be able to afford payment for their health care. In fact, such income redistribution and subsidies do exist now for those over 65 in Medicare B, the part that pays for doctors. Three quarters of the cost of Medicare

B comes out of general tax revenues which, to a large extent, derive from the wealthy and the upper middle class. They also exist for the disabled who are eligible for Medicare as well as for those on Medicaid, the health program for the poor, paid by the general revenue of the States and the Federal government.

These two programs involve redistribution and subsidies on the payment side. But obviously they also involve redistribution from the healthy to the sick.

Any group health plan will involve redistribution from the healthy to the sick. And, since the young generally require fewer health services than the older, there will also be a redistribution from the young to the older.

In summary, there can be redistribution on the payment side and there will be redistribution on the benefit side. Indeed, the latter is the principle of insurance.

The redistribution from the healthy to the sick has one obvious consequence. Younger people will be far more likely to stay out of the plans, i.e. not "buy" insurance, than those older. But this decreases the size of the risk pool and increases the average cost per participant, hence the premiums. That in turn means that the younger are then even more likely to stay out of such plans since the subsidies will go against them.

In the US, a comprehensive private/public health plan will, at the minimum, have to involve: (a) subsidies to low income households on the payment side; (b) a requirement that every US resident be a member of a health group, buying a stated minimum of health insurance with specific insurance coverage in order to maximize the risk pool; (c) a requirement that anyone has the right to enroll in any health group; (d) an equalization process between health groups, shifting some funds to those health groups with a higher proportion of older participants and/or participants with certain expensive diseases; (e) some deductibles and co-payments. (f) computerization of the whole system. Drug coverage should be included, as well as hospitalization and physician services.

Currently there are all kinds of inefficiencies built into the US health system. First, there is a vast amount of expensive paperwork. Large numbers of personnel are hired to contend with this veritable flood. This is true in doctor's offices; it is true in hospitals; it is true in insurance plans. More and more health professionals spend a larger and larger fraction of their working hours on insurance problems. All this runs up costs.

The large numbers of insurance plans, health maintenance organizations, and government programs, each with its own separate rules and treatment limitations, require extensive administrative procedures. The multiplicity of modest size risk pools means a multiplicity of cost structures and a multiplicity of payment plans, even if average coverage is very similar.

To be sure, there is now an effort to computerize all the paperwork more and more, but there is a long way to go. The basic problems will remain and will continue to require large numbers of personnel to contend with all these problems.

Second, there are very substantial unexplained differences in treatment for exactly the same ailments , and very substantial resulting cost differences, in different parts of the country. In some areas, there are very expensive procedures used to treat some conditions. In other areas simple and inexpensive treatments are in vogue. But there do not seem to be any consistently different outcomes. Clearly there will be commensurately different costs in different areas. Some of these differences appear to relate to profitability considerations, others are a mystery.

It also turns out that some procedures, such as heart surgery, tend to be more profitable than others, partly due to the size of the insurance or government reimbursements. The result has been the departure of groups of doctors from general hospitals to establish their own specialized hospitals. These are likely to be profitable, while the general hospitals lose an important profit center. In other words, incentives matter. Such perverse incentives should be remedied.

Third, there are serious problems of access to the health system. To be sure, anyone can go to the emergency room, a rather expensive way of getting treatment, without ever paying the bill. Hospitals are legally required to provide treatment in their emergency rooms to anyone and stabilize the patient, for obvious public policy reasons.

In essence, this is an unfunded mandate, with the hospital left with the unpaid costs. These costs will have to be recouped through higher charges to those capable of paying, transfers of funds from profitable sections of the hospital, special taxes imposed in some states on hospital bills of private payers, or charitable contributions. Hospitals that cannot manage will go bankrupt.

Other than the emergency room, the uninsured will have major difficulties in getting treatment. They will have to appeal to government and private programs designed to contend with these issues, such as Medicaid. But all of these programs are difficult of access, have limited funds, a great many rules, and often very partial coverage. Also they tend to require frequent reapplication and a large amount of confusing paperwork and documentation. This keeps many out.

Fourth, there is the subject of fraud. This is a particular problem in the Medicaid program and, to a lesser extent, in Medicare. But it also affects private insurance. Here, more resources have to be made available to investigate and prosecute those responsible.

Fifth, there is the problem of the so-called legacy costs - pensions and medical insurance costs of the retired, found in many older American companies, such as GM, Ford and airlines. Such companies are at a competitive disadvantage relative to other, more recently founded US companies with younger workers and fewer such plans for the retired. They are

Peter Gutmann

also at a disadvantage relative to foreign competitors where national health insurance pays the medical bill, A number of such older US companies with heavy legacy costs have gone bankrupt, extinguishing or reducing the company paid medical benefits of retired workers.

Sixth, there is the problem of defensive medicine, with many unnecessary tests, running up costs, to protect against potential lawsuits.

Seventh, and extremely important, the current growth rate of US health expenditures cannot continue indefinitely. There is bound to be some sort of health rationing as noted earlier. This will probably take the form of plans that are on the low side in terms of coverage.

Government plans will increasingly require larger direct payments for all participants, less coverage, and higher payments by high income recipients, with greater income redistribution on the payment side. The latter is already happening in Medicare.

The net result will be continuing need for private supplementary insurance to provide coverage where Medicare does not. In this respect, it should again be noted that supplementary private insurance is widely utilized in European countries that have a national health program. Some also have had restrictions on various procedures such as kidney dialysis, hip replacements for the high aged, etc.

Chapter 9

LEARNING

Learning is extremely important in any society, and particularly important in the advanced, industrialized countries where there is a heavy premium on the education, the technical skills and the capacity to run their complex economies. High levels of human capital are required to operate the high levels of real capital and the high levels of technology to produce high levels of immensely varied output. The US is the largest country by far where these conditions pertain.

But the US educational system required to produce these high levels of human capital has numerous problems and significantly fails to succeed in its objectives in all too many ways. Of course we do not have one educational system. We have thousands. Each state is different. Each city is different. Each of the multi thousands of school districts is different. They vary very widely in quality. The American system of public school financing is at the bottom of many of these problems. (This matter is covered in the chapter on "Access"). Attempts to impose minimum Federal standards have not been notably successful. Also the Federal minimum standards are quite different from the minimum standards of the various states.

Both the Federal and the States minimum standards aim at the bottom, not the top. They aim to bring the lowest performing students up to a minimum level. This means testing as well as teaching to the test. Recent decades have seen enormous efforts to upgrade the educational performance of those students furthest behind, while more or less letting top students fend for themselves.

To be sure, the upper level students, once they reach high school, can take advanced placement tests designed to equal college level work. But high schools in different districts vary tremendously in the number of such advanced placement tests actually offered. As for elite public high schools for the gifted, they tend to be confined to a modest number of cities, such as New York and Boston. The fraction of gifted students in the country at large with access to such schools is minuscule.

It turns out that these attempts to upgrade the bottom of the distribution are expensive, in many cases very expensive. This leaves fewer resources available for the average performing students, let alone the top layer. So, more funds are needed, funds that must compete with many other uses for such funds.

One very important problem in education is the tendency to pour everyone into the same bottle. The reality is that people are different. Students are different as well; their performance differs not only by student, but also by subject. To a large extent this is too often ignored by most educational systems.

The bane of teachers at all levels is this: heterogeneous classes. The teacher is left in the nigh impossible situation of trying to teach excellent, average, poor and even terrible students in the same classroom at the same time. What is the result? Most teachers will pitch themselves at some middle level. The top students become bored and perform far below their capacity. The bottom students get lost and fall behind. Now, with the emphasis on bringing bottom students up to minimum levels, the danger is that teachers will pitch themselves lower, hurting not only top students but also average students. More learning is lost as the result of heterogeneous classes than for just about any other reason in education.

What is needed is to divide students into more homogeneous groups in terms of learning capacity, homogeneous by subject. The top students will learn much more. The bottom students are much more likely to be brought up to minimum standards.

This is in fact done to a limited extent. But in the US there is a major problem. It is a social and political problem. It turns out, when there is a division into more homogeneous groups, that the top, middle and bottom groups generally do not include equal proportions of different ethnic groups. For this and other reasons, this division, commonly known as tracking, is not popular and often not politically acceptable in the public schools.

In recent years these problems have become even greater as more students in special education have been mainstreamed into regular classrooms. This may or may not be good for the children concerned, but all too frequently it is bad for the rest of the class as teachers, untrained to handle such children, struggle to prevent disruptions affecting the class as a whole.

So, a great deal of potential learning and human capital formation is lost. Clearly, ways ought to be found to overcome the objections to more widespread use of homogeneous groups.

Our system of education is particularly bad at mathematics and science. These are not easy subjects. Many students try to get away with the minimum. This shows up at the college and graduate school level in an inadequate number of majors in these subjects, as well as an inadequate number of candidates for higher degrees. As a result, the US must import a continuous flow of scientists and engineers from countries with better educational systems in the sciences and engineering, not only into our graduate schools as students, but also into the country as immigrants to fill out the needs of the US labor force.

41

Chapter 10

HOUSING

Somewhat more than two-thirds of Americans enjoy ownership of private houses, condominiums and coops. But there are problems, serious problems, both among households and in the macroeconomy at large.

First there is the matter of purchase affordability. Lower income households typically cannot afford to own their own home. Second, there are a great many who are devoting more than thirty per cent of their income for housing expenses. This is generally considered a rather high figure. Some are even devoting more than fifty per cent of their income to housing costs. Third, innumerable local zoning and construction requirements make housing unnecessarily expensive in many areas and many jurisdictions also prevent use of more efficient and less expensive manufactured housing as opposed to housing built fully at the site. Fourth, from the macroeconomic point of view, housing construction shows very substantial fluctuations. These affect the macroeconomy in positive and negative ways.

Most of the lowest portion of the income distribution, i.e. the poor, not to mention those in actual poverty, can scarcely afford purchase of a house or condominium. Most will never be able to afford one. Houses and apartments are simply too expensive, too expensive to buy and too expensive to run. The poor are largely confined to renting. And what they can rent is all too often of the worst quality.

Many in this large section of the population need help either for purchase or for rentals. The vast majority of such help in the past has come from a variety of governmental programs. But in recent years such government programs have clearly been on a downward trend. Programs of this type have lost popularity. Some of the past programs, particularly those involving high rise structures for the poor, have worked out badly. Realistically, the outlook for more adequate housing for low income recipients is not good.

A second group of households, particularly the lower and to some extent the middle of the middle class, are straining mightily to pay the bills. These are the households devoting more than thirty per cent of their income to pay housing expenses, both ownership and rental.

The drive to ownership in America is particularly strong. It is a major part of the American dream. So, many buy houses they can barely afford, even with two wage earners in the family. When one loses his or her job, or contracts a serious illness, disaster strikes. This whole group is at high risk.

Third, the numerous local zoning and construction requirements have the effect of increasing housing prices. These restrictions tend to drive up both land costs and construction costs, making housing less available. Land costs rise due to the restrictive zoning. Housing construction costs rise both because of local zoning requirements and because of inability to use factory built homes utilizing less expensive and lower skilled labor, in favor of construction at the site with higher cost higher skilled local labor. Zoning very often also excludes apartment buildings.

There is probably not much that can be done to ameliorate these problems due to the multiplicity of jurisdictions as well as numerous local issues. It would require state as well as local action. This is none too likely in the overwhelming majority of districts around the country. The high price of housing in so many areas of the country has been a particular problem for the young.

Fourth are the macroeconomic issues. In the mid decade, housing construction was running not far from five per cent of the GDP. In the preceding half a dozen years it had risen substantially as a proportion of US GDP. More recently, of course, it has been in major decline.

These large fluctuations in the important housing sector have a very significant impact on total demand for US output. An increase is very favorable for the economy and a decrease very unfavorable, due to the size of the sector. This sector has been particularly important in recent years due to the need to compensate for the negative demand created by the US import surplus, as US purchasing power spills out of the country. This negative demand has to be made up by the other elements of US total demand, of which housing is a significant part.

Housing construction is a very substantial part of total US investment. For example, in mid decade it was running at about half of the construction sector - residential, commercial and government, a large share of total investment. Total investment demand in turn plus consumption demand and net government demand comprise the three elements that have to compensate for the gigantic negative demand in our foreign trade. So, a drop in housing construction can act as a blow to the economy at large.

On top of these issues came the combined liquidity crisis, credit crunch, confidence crisis and rediscovery of risk in the summer of 2007. This derived initially from the abuses in housing finance in the sub prime sector where poor credit risks were granted large mortgage loans that a great many could not afford and would eventually not be able to repay. Low initial mortgage interest rates as well as very low down payments were used as bait. These interest rates were scheduled to reset later at much higher variable rates, that jumped monthly payments to much higher levels.

These high interest rates and the accompanying higher monthly payments were beyond the financial capacity of many sub prime borrowers. Result: rising delinquency and rising foreclosures; decline in the market value of the underlying mortgages that had been collected in mortgage pools sliced into different risk segments; spread of financial market deterioration to the alt-A mortgages; and from there to many other financial assets backed by housing paper. Markets seized up, ability to sell rapidly diminished, and near panic ensued in more or less the entire bond and note markets other than US and some foreign Treasury paper and its near kin. Finally the Fed and the European Central Bank stepped in, provided lots of money to provide liquidity, and the Fed reduced its discount rate, encouraged banks to borrow from it, and then reduced the Federal Funds rate.

In retrospect numerous financial investors bitterly regretted their preceding cavalier treatment of the subject of risk. It proved an expensive fault. A risk shift occurred, as risk suddenly became more expensive. With more focus on risk, many asset prices declined more or less permanently. Housing prices went south. It has also become evident that only about two-thirds of Americans are in a financial position to be homeowners. Given the existing structure of the economy, much expansion beyond that point is simply not feasible. On top of that, mortgages are likely to be harder to get, with bigger down payments, and interest rates somewhat more expensive relative to other long term obligations, in the next few years.

Chapter 11

THE WORLD OF WORK

The world of work has changed drastically in recent decades. It has changed with rapid advances in technology, rapid industrialization of Asian economies and rapid globalization.

No longer is there any assurance of a lifetime job in a single company in the private sector. The company itself has to change far too rapidly just to survive, let alone guarantee any particular kind of job. And, indeed, the company may not be around for the full working lifetime of all of its employees. The assumption of eternal corporate life may not hold these days.

This means that just about every employee in the private sector has to be prepared to have multiple jobs in a lifetime. This requires great labor flexibility - maximum flexibility in skill transfer, maximum flexibility in health benefit transfer, maximum flexibility in geographic mobility, maximum flexibility in pension transfer. We have not achieved full flexibility in all these sectors by any means, particularly on the health side.

It also requires continuous skill enhancement, in effect perpetual retraining. As the nature of the jobs changes, the skills of those in the jobs must also change. Failure to keep up tends to result in dropouts from the labor force or in drop downs into less desirable and less well paying jobs.

The ability to benefit from retraining, i.e. from additional education, is related to the amount of basic education the employee has acquired in the past in primary and secondary school, college and other educational programs on and off the job. Considering that 70 per cent don't even graduate from high school, there is a large, woeful gap in our basic educational system. That then manifests itself years later in poor capacity to adjust in rapidly changing labor markets, in higher unemployment, lower income, dropouts from the labor force and poor adjustment to our changing world.

It also results in far too many dropouts from the middle class into the land of the poor, far too many bankruptcies, and far too much plain misery. Failure in basic education is difficult to make up later, as shown in many remedial programs.

In addition we have to recognize a profound truth when we consider that the current generation is the first generation not better educated than their parents.

Flexibility in the labor market is impeded by a number of factors. First is the lack of portability of health benefits. Many workers are reluctant to change jobs because they cannot carry their health benefits with them to a new and different employer. This is a major matter. In fact, it is a critical matter to many, particularly older workers who are more likely to require medical intervention. Of course, under current law, anyone leaving an employer can continue for three years to pay for the benefits out of their own pocket. But this is no substitute. In point of fact, many cannot afford this, particularly if their state of health precludes easy access to another job.

Second, is the matter of pension portability. This has both improved and become worse in different ways. It has improved with the introduction and spread of 401(k) accounts and similar plans which belong to the employee and can be carried anywhere. These are called defined contribution plans. It has also improved because workers do not have to wait until they are vested (i.e. have to wait for a stated number of years to own all the assets in the plans). But it has also worsened because employer contributions to these plans are usually less than their effective employer contributions to the older, defined benefit pension plans which have been discontinued by many employers.

Third, and very important, is the subject of adequate, flexible skills. The better the skill set, the more flexible is the worker in all respects. This harkens back to education and training.

Fourth, labor market flexibility is affected by the willingness of workers to move to a different part of the country. This is far less of an issue here than in Europe where matters such as dialect and language are much greater. But flexibility is affected by rent controlled apartments that cannot be duplicated elsewhere, houses that are difficult to sell at a reasonable price, and of course family considerations.

We then come to the matter of retirement. Continuation of work to old age was made possible years ago through Federal legislation abolishing a stated retirement age. But..jobs have to be available. This is ordinarily not a problem in areas such as academic life, but it is a serious problem in many companies where internal changes, often connected with technological change and/or globalization, result in substantial layoffs of many workers. As a result, particularly workers in their fifties or above find themselves looking for acceptable jobs in vain.

They then wind up in an effective early retirement, often beset by uncovered medical expenses prior to eligibility for Medicare, as well as by other financial problems. Programs to assist these people are either inadequate or wholly nonexistent. Corporations are increasingly abandoning this group of ex-employees. In those cases where there are still such corporate programs they are being cut back, require more individual payments or are on the way out.

Peter Gutmann

There is now increasing political pressure to assist this group and their financial obligations, including health coverage in the transitional years prior to availability of Medicare.

Chapter 12

RETIREMENT AND PENSIONS

The major problems of financing retirement may be summarized thus: we work for too few years and are out of the workforce for too many; we consume too much and save too little of our income; we have historically taken too much of increased productivity in terms of leisure; the lowest two fifths of the income distribution cannot afford to save at all; our ability to even conceive of the financing needs for retirement many years hence is extremely limited; we put present needs first and retirement needs last; we don't listen to retirement financing experts.

The result is obvious. When the evil day comes that we look at our assets and realize that they are wholly inadequate to finance retirement, it is typically too late in life to resolve the problem. We are then stuck with an inadequate income flow in the retirement years. Many have little more than low Social Security receipts. Lots become dependent on government programs and charity, eventually winding up in nursing homes financed at government expense through Medicaid. Others have to go back to work. Still others become a burden to their children.

In contrast, those who prepare adequately through lifetime accumulation of assets that can be liquidated during the retirement years, will enjoy well financed retirements. This includes the rich and those in the middle class who have both the foresight and the means to accumulate assets while working.

Retirement is a phase of life that has been lengthening with the increasing life span of the population. As a result, it is getting more and more expensive. This increasing expense has to be financed during the working years.

So, at least in principle, a larger and larger fraction of earnings during the working years has to be set aside to build the equity that will be used up during the retirement years. But the working years are also very expensive years - housing, children, education, medical, insurance, cars, transportation, taxes and a thousand other costs eat up available income. As a result, US household savings rates have not been much above zero for years and are currently actually negative.

And so the savings needed for a reasonable retired lifestyle have not been forthcoming from much of the private sector. Of course there are the government programs. Yet, Social Security was never designed to cover full retirement costs. And, for most people, Social Security payments are quite modest, in keeping with their modest working year income. These payments are inadequate, even in the less expensive parts of the country. To be sure, Medicare becomes available at 65 and serves to cover most medical expenses. But even here, supplementary insurance is necessary.

This brings us back to the private sector financing of retirement during the working years. Starting with the World War II years, the so-called defined benefit pensions were adopted by many major private sector employers, as a means of attracting and retaining employees, as a substitute for raises which were highly restricted or impossible under wartime regulations. Essentially these defined benefit plans were contracts between employers and (largely unionized) workers to pay pensions after retirement, the amounts dependent on the number of years worked in the company and the income made during those years. It was really an agreement between company and workers to pay part of their income after retirement. In other words, it was a form of forced savings during the working years, that then became an annuity during the retirement years.

There were many problems in the administration of these programs over the years. Some were underfunded, others were overfunded at various times. And the whole notion of under or over funding was dependent on many assumptions as to future interest rates, future life expectancies and other factors. On top of all that, some of these programs were far too heavily invested in the stock and bonds of the company itself, a very risky investment strategy. Where funds were "overfunded" based on all these assumptions, whether realistic or not, the company took back large sums into its own coffers.

There was also the basic assumption that the company would still be around and in reasonably good shape when the pension payments became due. Unfortunately this was not always the case. A number of large bankruptcies came in steel, airlines and other, mostly older, industries. In those cases, the Pension Benefit Guaranty Corporation, set up by the government, took over the pension funds and most of their obligations. It then made the promised pension payments, but only up to a maximum amount per person. So, highly paid employees in this situation lost out.

The Pension Benefit Guaranty Corporation itself, inundated with bankruptcies, was vastly underfunded and became more than twenty billions under water, i.e. negative equity. If an auto company goes under, the Federal Government will have a huge bailout of the Pension Benefit Guarantee Corporation on its hands, quite possibly of similar magnitude to the Savings and Loan bailout of the 1980s eventually. Still, most companies will not go bankrupt.

For a great many of the companies with the defined benefit plans, the so-called legacy costs (pensions and medical) have become a real burden, particularly if the companies are shrinking in size. This has become very obvious, notably in the widely publicized cases of GM and Ford. So, such companies have been extremely anxious to shed these plans or at least reduce them and stop accepting new members.

At the same time, in the last couple of decades, there has been a strong movement towards more individual responsibility for decisions on pensions. The old defined benefit plans are being replaced by defined contribution plans. The 401(k) and similar plans have taken over. The pensions in these plans are owned by the participant and are portable from one employer to another. In these plans the participant chooses from among a number of different investment portfolios.

Currently, new employees in a participating firm will be enrolled automatically in such a plan unless they choose to opt out. This reverses the previous system where new employees had to opt into the plan. This change is definitely expected to increase participation in these savings plans. Under the new law, employers set contribution levels in their 401(k) plan to at least 3 per cent of salaries and permit automatic escalation to a maximum of 6 per cent by the fourth year. Companies must match at a rate of a least 2 per cent but not more than 3.5 per cent.

But the change from opting in to opting out still does not require absolute compulsion to participate, since it is possible to opt out. So, it is not quite compulsory saving. Furthermore, the funds in the 401(k)s can be taken out by their owners in a lump sum (with a 10 per cent penalty if done before age 59 1/2). That further reduces the compulsory savings feature. Still, it is an advance in pension planning. But, the only way to guarantee availability of funds for pensions is to make contributions compulsory and withdrawals before the day when the pension actually starts exceedingly difficult. Of course Social Security works that way with no possibility to make early withdrawals prior to the age of

62. In the 401(k)s, the participant has a choice of investment vehicles.

Americans are wonderful consumers but poor savers. Most of us want instant gratification, the latest gadgets, he latest movies, the latest cars, the most meals in restaurants, bigger houses and apartments, and so forth. The result is a low or nonexistent household savings rate as well as low provision for pensions. If the savings rate is ever to increase more than marginally, there will have to be a greater element of compulsion in savings. Individual responsibility has failed to do the job.

There is one other element in financing retirement that is relevant, namely the house. A little more than two-thirds of Americans own their own home or, better said, what is left of the home after the first and second mortgages, and the used part of the equity lines of credit with the home as security. There has been so much borrowing, so much remortgaging with cash taken out that many retirees find that a sale of the house does not go very far in financing their retirement. Yes, there is still a very large equity in American homes, but the distribution is very uneven, leaving many with only modest amounts.

Chapter 13

ENERGY

All energy on earth can be traced back to the nuclear reactions in the sun. It comes to us every day and has come to us for billions of years. It is incorporated in the plant and animal life of the planet, past and present. Coal, oil, natural gas, water power, all come from the energy emanating from the sun.

Just about every economy requires large amounts of energy to run smoothly. But practically every economy could get along with a lot less energy. Much of current world discussion of energy relates to the reduction of waste and inefficiency in the use of energy. In recent decades this has been complicated by the recognition that most energy use by far increases the amount of carbon dioxide in the air, leading to global warming. This has created enormous interest in forms of energy that do not create carbon dioxide.

Major uses of energy are: transportation; electric power production including air conditioning use; and heating. In the US, our use of energy has been fairly exotic over the years, with still inadequate focus on efficiency and waste. Despite all the attention to energy in recent decades, government mandates, incentives and tax policies have been inadequate to truly come to grips with excessive use of energy. Price increases in gasoline, for example, have helped a little, but US gas prices at the pump are still far below those in Europe.

The Europeans have used tax policy to make energy much more expensive, thus depending on the resulting increases in the cost of energy to reduce usage. When a driver pulls up at a filling station in Europe,and buys gasoline or diesel, most of the cost of each liter lies in the taxes levied by governments. Yes, we too have taxes on gasoline - Federal taxes, state taxes, sales taxes - but they are so small relative to those in Europe that their effect on usage is minimal.

Then there is the matter of mandatory minimum miles per gallon standards imposed on auto manufacturers. The US had done practically nothing on that score for many years until Congress finally woke up in the summer of 2007 to legislate enhanced minimum mileage standards.

Home heating is another example. President Carter once recommended wearing a sweater. He was laughed out of court. But in fact this minor adjustment is quite sensible. To be sure, better insulation and better windows have helped, but Americans are still reluctant to turn down the thermostat. The Federal Government not only doesn't tax home heating oil like gasoline. It exempts it from taxes.

In the meantime, our import bill for petroleum and natural gas products is rising inexorably. Due to reduction in the proportion of our needs filled by domestic production, the quantity of petroleum product imports has been increasing for many years. And in the last couple of years, the price per barrel went up substantially. The net result is a rising import bill that forms a substantial portion of our huge and unsustainable import surplus.

The pressure is on to find substitutes, particularly domestic substitutes, for gasoline. In Brazil this has been done successfully with ethanol from sugar cane. The US is not exactly replete with sugar cane, but ethanol could be made out of sugar beets. We use corn. But to produce ethanol from corn, you have to use about a gallon of petroleum products to produce one and a half gallons of ethanol. This is a very low ratio. In Brazil, the ratio from sugarcane is about eight to one. But, never mind. There is now a mad rush for corn and a mad rush to invest in plants producing ethanol from corn. This rush increased corn prices initially, followed by increased plantings and corn price drop again. Acreage for other crops was reduced. All this then affected food prices.

The use of energy in producing electricity has created a conundrum for many. The only practical large scale alternative that does not produce carbon dioxide, other than water power which has already been largely exploited, is nuclear power. But nuclear power has not been popular in the US, unlike France which gets most of its electricity from nuclear power. We haven't built a new nuclear power plant within the US for decades. Still, the global warming issue is changing the opinion of at least some of the green organizations slowly as they face the dichotomy of power and carbon dioxide. Others pin their hopes on minor sources of electric power such as wind power and solar power. But nearly all of them are working to conserve electricity so that fewer new power stations are needed in the first place.

It does look like some US nuclear power stations will be built in the next decade or two. Of course security considerations will have to be overcome. Still, most new power stations are likely to be coal - some perhaps with yet untested technology to store carbon dioxide underground.

There is no doubt that the US is behind in saving on energy use. The outlook though is that efficiency will increase and waste will be reduced. The outlook on carbon dioxide emission, short of nuclear plants, is less promising.

PART 4: PERSONAL RISK

Chapter 14

INCREASE IN PERSONAL RISK: ANXIETY OF THE PUBLIC

The changing American economy is piling more and more risk onto the substantial majority of the population. Most of the public doesn't like it. It creates a great deal of anxiety. Some of this increase in risk is inevitable and worldwide. Other components are US based and can be reduced.

Much of this increase in risk is particularly worrisome to the average person because it is a risk that can result in a drop out of the middle class into poverty. That worry is never very far from the minds of tens of millions.

The most obvious increase in risk has come with the decrease in job security. In the old days, many went to work with their employers after high school or college and stayed with that same employer for life. No more. Today, the average employee in the private sector has multiple employers in a lifetime. When there is a job loss, particularly if accompanied by poor health, there is always the risk of bankruptcy

There are many reasons for decreased job security. Corporations themselves face a riskier environment, a more competitive environment, with new competitors emerging out of unsuspected corners. Today they are forced far more often into restructuring, downsizing, layoffs, mass firings, relocations, outsourcing, mergers and rapid technological change. Many older corporations also face huge legacy costs - pension obligations, rising medical insurance expenses as their work force ages, and aging plant and equipment. All of these also increase job insecurity and personal employee risk. This kind of risk increase is part and parcel of a rapidly changing world - technological, domestic, global.

There is also the risk of sudden, high medical expenses. These too can send the unfortunate victim into bankruptcy and out of the middle class. In the old days many large employers footed the bill for medical insurance in full or almost in full. Now, employees pay a larger and larger share of the bill for insurance that may not even cover their families. Deductions and co-payments are also rising. And employees of small business in particular are likely to have no medical insurance at all.

Many other industrialized countries have solved at least the major part of this risk problem through universal health insurance, but of course at the cost of higher business and personal taxes to finance these plans. This seems unlikely in the US in the foreseeable near future for those under 65, with the exception of Medicaid and programs for children.

Still another risk associated problem is the subject of pensions and other income after retirement. Corporations have been steadily reducing or abandoning fixed benefit type pensions. Instead, there are now a variety of plans that are contributory by employees. Employers may also contribute to them. These generally have fixed contributions once a plan is selected and then are invested in the private sector in the bond, stock and real estate markets, subject to the vagaries of market fluctuations. So, the specific amount of the pension is not known until the date of retirement.

Social Security, established in the 1930's, does have a fixed relationship between annual contributions and the actual pension. This relationship is set by the Social Security law. It is subject to change by legislation. Technically the Social Security tax is paid equally by employers and employees, but most economists agree that the actual burden is on the employee (since employers otherwise would add their Social Security contributions to wages and salaries).

It is a very popular program. The attempt by the Bush Administration to convert part of it into a riskier program through investment of the contributions in the private sector met with howls of protest and eventually had to be dropped. It failed in good measure because the Administration wanted to introduce risk while most of the public wanted no part of increased risk.

About the only job related way these days to avoid most of the risks associated with job loss, health insurance and private pensions is to work for the Federal, State and Local Governments or their Agencies, or many universities. These generally provide "permanent jobs", that is to say some sort of tenure. Government jobs are nowadays the goal of many since they are far less risky and often pay relatively well. In Europe, the goal of a "permanent job" is even more avidly sought than it is in the US.

On the subject of medical insurance and pensions, governments - Federal, State and Local - can do much to reduce personal risk. A certain amount has been done already.

The introduction and enhancement of the 401(k) individual pension programs in corporations has made pensions portable since they belong to employees, but at the cost of a the risk implicit in a defined contribution as opposed to a defined benefit pension program. Also, corporate contributions to these tend to be smaller than they were under the old defined benefit programs. For the older pension plans, where there was always the possibility of corporate bankruptcy, the establishment of the

Pension Benefit Guarantee Corporation (now in difficulties) as a guarantor of the affected pensions, was clearly an advance.

On the subject of Social Security, payments could be raised for the lower income groups by abandoning the current maximum income levels for FICA contributions (which has already been done for Medicare contributions) and changing the legislated relationship between contributions and benefits for the upper income contributors.

On the side of medical insurance, a couple of states, such as Massachusetts and California, either have an operational program designed to provide near universal medical insurance for state residents or are seriously studying proposals for such a program. A major difficulty is the high cost and, hence, problems of financing such programs. There are still other possibilities for risk reduction in the medical field. For example, a group much at risk are those not yet eligible for medicare who no longer are covered by employer based medical insurance. These could be largely covered by lowering the age for medical coverage below 65, say to 60, for this group.

There are also specific technological change type of job related risks in today's world of rapid technological change. Workers and employees lose jobs all the time due to inability to handle the new technologies that the changing jobs require.

The use of computers everywhere requires familiarity with a variety of software programs, some easy to learn, others very difficult. Since younger workers tend to be more adept at learning new computer skills it is often the older worker who is more at risk - older engineers, older technicians, older computer based workers at every level. This is true for practically all changing technologies.

The solution to technological risks, risks of worker obsolescence, is intensive training in newer technologies at every level and age. Since it will not pay private sector corporations to do all of this, subsidies by government are going to be required and continue to be required for many of such educational programs.

PART 5: THE MACROECONOMY

Chapter 15

EATING THE HOUSE

For years there have been innumerable complaints about the lack of savings by American households. The savings ratio of US households has been declining more or less steadily over a decade. It has reached the point where household savings are essentially zero, sometimes a little above, sometimes a little below. Currently they are less than zero.

Developments in the housing area have played a very large role in the overall decline in the household savings ratio. In recent times, there has been so much borrowing on the equity ownership of homes, followed by spending a good part of that borrowing, i.e. negative savings, that the overall national household savings rate breached the zero level on the way down.

Financial innovations in the mortgage business made it far easier to borrow on the security of homes. At the same time, the runup in the value of homes in most areas of the country during the first half decade of the millennium greatly increased the value of the equity in housing on which to borrow.

So, in recent years, the combination of easier access to mortgages, easier ways to acquire second mortgages, easier ways to get a line of credit on the security of homes, rising home prices and a long period of low mortgage rates have stimulated such a large amount of borrowing on homes, that the resulting amounts of negative savings swamped the positive savings elsewhere in the economy among the higher income groups, to yield a net household savings rate of less than zero.

There is good reason to believe that rising mortgage rates, lower availability, and tougher down payment requirements, combined with the end of high housing appreciation, will reduce the amount of negative savings due to remortgaging and, hence, result in a net positive savings rate in the future. Some of this may well occur, but there are no guarantees. There remains an enormous amount of equity in the housing market, and an enormous borrowing potential. That, combined with the very high American proclivity for instant consumer satisfaction, will guarantee continued relatively high borrowing on home ownership, even though less than before, and so continue relatively high negative savings originating in the housing sector.

This is an often discussed problem in the economy. However it is a two edged sword. True, the low, nonexistent or negative household savings rate has been a vanishing counterpart to capital formation. And it has driven up the proportion of the GDP that is consumption, as opposed to investment. It also puts us among the lowest savings rate countries in the world.

But, there has also been a positive result. With our enormous import surplus and the spillage of so much of US demand outside the country, the increase in domestic consumption due to the remortgaging boom, helped plug this hole so far. So the decline in household saving, i.e. the increase in household consumption, served to prop up domestic demand and helped to prevent an early recession.

But the long term effect is evident. With more of the GDP in consumption and less in investment, the growth of the productive capital stock is less. In addition, the increase in the size of the housing sector meant that a larger proportion of US investment has been in private housing and a lesser proportion in other types of investment such as industrial, commercial, agricultural, etc. So there came to be a larger proportion in less productive and a smaller proportion in more productive investment. But housing investment declined substantially in the past year.

Fortunately, at least since the mid-nineties, the degree of technological innovation incorporated in the more productive types of investment - both net investment and replacement investment - has been very high. As a result, this degree of enhanced technological change compensated for the shift to private housing, and for the decline in household savings, from the economic growth point of view. But there is some question whether this will continue at a similar pace, or will slow down to more long term trends.

So, the average American is among the best housed in the world with a very high amount of living space per person, and with an extremely high ratio of consumption to income. But the average hides a great deal of variation in different groups. There are substantial problems in the distribution of such results, discussed elsewhere in this book.

What of the future? Financial innovations that make it easier to borrow on the security of the home will continue, even if modified. Reverse mortgages, for example, are growing at a good pace in numbers and amounts. These are designed to allow the elderly to stay in their own homes for a longer period of time, or until death, They are essentially a system of liquidating the equity in the house through monthly cash payments to the owners on an annuity basis. Slowly the owners are eating the house. Negative savings for them continue.

But those who count the house as a substitute for a pension may be sorely disappointed If they have been busily converting the house into consumption through the years with remortgaging, second mortgages, lines of credit, etc., there may not be much equity left when it comes to retirement.

All this has an effect on inheritance. Years ago, children counted on inheriting the house. Since mortgages were often paid off, the equity was simply the value of the house. No longer. Today, the reverse mortgages are growing in number. And even without them, the equity is often far less than the market value of the house due to remortgaging, second mortgages, and lines of credit that have been maxed out. The inheritance shrinks. This is common among the middle classes. Only the wealthy escape. For many, there is little or nothing left to be inherited.

Chapter 16

DEMAND FOR NATIONAL OUTPUT

To achieve high national output, high employment and low unemployment, there has to be high national demand to purchase this output. If such high national demand is not forthcoming, the economy will run at a lower level and may fall into recession.

In this respect, the US has a serious problem that might even get worse before it gets permanently better, even though it has improved a small amount recently. In any case the essential problem will continue for many years. The problem is our huge import surplus, running at around 6 per cent of national output. Imports have been more than half as much again as exports.

This import surplus means that a substantial portion of US demand spills outside the country and is not available to purchase US produced goods and services. This demand loss then has to be made up by a combination of US domestic consumer demand, US domestic investment demand and/ or the net government demand generated by an excess of government expenditures over government receipts.

For the US it is extremely difficult to reduce imports. Americans just love foreign produced goods as well as services such as tourism abroad. In addition, today even "American made" goods very often contain significant foreign components. This part of globalization has been built into the structure of American industry. Automobiles are a good example. And, over the years, more and more goods that formerly were made domestically have migrated to foreign production. Apparel, textiles, footwear and numerous other manufactures are now imported in massive quantities. US consumers are more than happy with all the inexpensive electronics, clothing and shoes from abroad.

To make it even more difficult, what is a problem for the US is the solution to a problem for foreign countries. A number of important foreign countries do not have enough internally generated demand to keep their economies humming at a high level. They need an export surplus to make up the shortfall. The US import surplus provides an enormous amount of externally generated demand for these countries. China is a case in point. It is heavily dependent on externally generated demand, particularly the US import surplus. Although China is now trying to raise its home demand, it will almost certainly continue to be dependent on net foreign demand, i.e. an export surplus, for its goods for years to come.

Of course the US import surplus depends in part on the exchange rate of the dollar. A cheaper dollar means that imports are more expensive and exports are less expensive. In fact, the decline in the exchange value of the dollar in recent years has served to increase our exports, thus reducing the import surplus at least somewhat as a proportion of GDP.

Further decline of our overvalued dollar would be favorable for the economy since it is likely to reduce our gigantic import surplus. This is particularly true relative to the undervalued Chinese renmimbi. But many foreign countries want to maintain a low value of their own currencies, hence a high value of the dollar, to keep up maximum exports and benefit from maximum foreign demand. This is particularly true of countries like China which places economic development above all other priorities.

These countries accomplish this objective through very large purchases of dollars by their central banks in the foreign exchange markets, selling their own currencies for dollars to keep them low and keep the dollar high. In the absence of such purchases the dollar would drop. Such a drop, in turn, as already noted, would reduce our import surplus at least to some degree. There has been a modest effect along these lines already due to the existing degree of reduction in the value of the dollar.

As long as foreign central banks intervene in the dollar exchange market by purchasing dollars, we can say that the dollar is overvalued, as it surely is today. But this does not mean that the absence of such foreign central bank intervention would result in disappearance of the import surplus. As long as there is a net demand for dollars to buy American assets on private international account, we will continue to have an import surplus, albeit a smaller one.

So, where does that leave US policy makers? It leaves them pleading with the Chinese to allow the renmimbi to rise faster relative to the dollar. Quite a number of US missions have made pilgrimages to Beijing already to plead our case. But US options are limited. Short of exploding the international trading system, for example by high tariffs let alone import quotas (which invite retaliation), in order to truncate our imports, there is not a great deal that can be done. We are also restricted by international agreements.

In the meantime, the macroeconomic effect on the US economy of the very large negative demand that is the import surplus still has to be faced for years to come. The larger the import surplus, the more difficult that will be. Failure to successfully contend with the negative macroeconomic effect of the import surplus, is likely to result in a less than full employment economy and possible recession.

So, how can we be reasonably assured of an adequate demand to compensate for the negative demand of the import surplus? Clearly, the sum total of the three other parts of total demand - consumption demand, investment demand and the demand generated by the difference between government expenditure and government receipts - has to compensate.

Through 2006, this was largely accomplished through very high consumer demand plus the investment demand generated by high level of housing construction. Household savings fell into negative territory when consumption exceeded household income. This high level of consumption, in turn, was heavily dependent on liquidation of some of the equity households held in their homes through remortgaging and cash outs. A good deal of the cash was spent on consumption. In addition, high housing demand combined with easy mortgage availability kept housing construction high.

This process was further encouraged by rapidly rising home prices in many parts of the country in the first half of the decade, increasing the magnitude of home equity. Further, low mortgage interest rates, low down payments, greater availability of sub prime mortgages, low "teaser" rates for the first couple of repayment years, and interest only mortgages, all tended to reduce monthly interest and repayment rates and increase housing demand.

However, these temporary, if risky, favorable circumstances broke down in 2006. Housing prices stopped rising and started falling in more and more areas. Mortgage rates tended up. But there was one favorable element, the huge amount of equity still remaining in private housing. On top of that, though, more and more easy, if dubious, mortgages were made available in the sub prime market, also holding up housing demand.

It looked increasingly like a bubble. And the bubble went into an amazingly very slow, prolonged deflation that finally gave way with a huge bang in August of 2007. A liquidity crisis, a credit crisis, a confidence crisis and a risk shift, all wrapped into one, blew up. The credit markets stopped working, holders of liquidity ran to the exits of short term Treasury debt which went well below the Federal funds rate. Even some commercial paper could not be sold. The Fed had to step in to prevent panic. Needless to say, this had a negative effect on both the demand for houses and consumer demand in general.

So, from a public policy viewpoint, how can the economy be kept operating at a high demand level when intervention becomes desirable and/or necessary? There are four elements of demand - consumer demand, investment demand, net foreign demand (a big negative) and net government demand.

It is domestic investment demand that should be stimulated. More investment implies higher productivity growth, the factor that permits long run increases in living standards. This has been done in the past and will be done again in the future. A time limited investment tax credit is perhaps the most obvious policy. It will cost some government tax revenue. This can be made up through taxes focused on the higher income groups, especially the very highest subgroup, the very groups that have benefited by the substantial shift in income distribution towards these groups in the last couple of decades.

What of consumption, the largest element of demand? Consumption, as a per cent of GDP, has been at a historical high with negative overall household savings. It makes sense to lower the proportion of consumption in the economy. The middle income group will probably have to cut back consumption somewhat due to less remortgaging of houses. This will reduce the negative savings implicit when a good part of the cash is spent. The upper income groups, faced with higher taxes, will also reduce consumption. The net result will be a reduction in consumption made up by an increase in investment.

On the side of foreign trade, a lower value of the dollar would increase exports, decrease imports, lower the import surplus, i.e. lower the current huge negative demand as spillage of purchasing out of the country is reduced. This is highly desirable. Since a negative number is being reduced, it has the effect of increasing overall demand. It would be helpful if the Administration could stop talking out of both halves of its mouth. On the one hand, Secretary Paulson, and before him Secretary Snow, made many speeches advocating a strong dollar. On the other they led missions to persuade China to increase the dollar value of the renmimbi, i.e. reduce the value of the dollar. The truth of the matter is that our overvalued dollar should go down in value.

The fourth element of demand, net government demand, the difference between government revenues and expenditures, will have to be kept flexible to contend with unexpected developments. It should be noted again that the tax increases on the upper income groups will increase revenue while the stimulation of investment will decrease revenue.

The combination of pursuing desirable policy options while, at the same time, keeping the economy on an even keel by maintaining high domestic demand, will not be easy. Fortunately the flexibility of the American economy helps a great deal.

Chapter 17

INCREASE IN SAVINGS; DECREASE IN GOVERNMENT DEFICIT: PROBLEMS OR SOLUTIONS?

An increase in household savings, i.e. a decrease in consumption, and a decrease in the government deficit have two things in common: both result in decreased national demand and both release resources that could be used elsewhere in the economy.

They also have something else in common. Both are solutions to problems at some times and actual problems at other times. It all depends on the state of the economy at particular times.

Unfortunately, much of the discussions of these subjects is carried on in terms of absolutes. Much is ideological and based on faith rather than cogent economic analysis. Much fails to recognize the time dependency of proper policies in regard to these two issues. As a result improper and harmful policies are pursued at times. This can do damage to the economy.

An increase in savings releases resources that otherwise would be used to produce consumer goods and services for households. A decrease in the government deficit due to a decrease in government expenditures releases resources that otherwise would be used to produce goods and services taken by government. A decrease in the government deficit due to an increase in taxes releases resources that otherwise would be taken by those taxpayers.

Any policy that increases the release of resources can be a proper policy if the resources so released are actually put to work. If they simply languish in idleness, then it becomes an improper policy.

There are only three other areas where such resources released by an increase in savings can be applied: business investment, foreign trade (increase in exports or substitution for imports) and use by government. So it all depends whether the business sector, the foreign trade sector or the government sector are willing and able to use such resources. If they are not, then the released resources will be idle and unemployed. That is obviously wasteful.

Similarly, there are only three areas where resources released by a decrease in the government deficit can be applied: business investment, foreign trade and use by consumers. So it all depends whether the business sector, the foreign trade sector or the household sector are willing and able to use such resources. If they are not, then the released resources will be idle and unemployed. That, again, is wasteful.

Generally speaking, when the economy is in high gear, such released resources are likely to be productively utilized. That includes labor. When the economy is in low gear, such released resources probably will not find employment.

The release of resources is a solution to a problem when there is an economic boom and a shortage of resources. For example, a policy that leads to a reduction in the government deficit through reduction in government expenditures would be a proper policy So would be a policy that led to an increase in savings, i.e. a reduction in consumption. For example, this might be accomplished by some types of real savings incentives such as stimulation of 401(k)s for middle income employees.

All these would not be good policies if the economy is in a slump.

A particularly difficult problem right now is the existence of our vary large import surplus. Some 6 per cent of demand is spilling out of the country, This 6 per cent has disappeared from demand for goods and services produced domestically. It is a negative demand. It has had to be counterbalanced by very high consumer demand, investment demand and the difference between government expenditures and receipts.

Any increase in savings or decrease in the government deficit at such times threatens to reduce total national demand, unless counterbalanced by an increase in the other two elements of total demand. These other two are: first, an increase in business investment demand; and, second, a decrease in the import surplus, i.e. an increase in exports or a decrease in imports, to reduce the negative demand as purchasing power spills out of the country.

So, increase in saving and decrease in the government deficit can be good or bad at particular times, depending on the specific macroeconomic problems at such times. There are no absolutes.

In the long run, looking forward for many years, there are still other issues. Governments are likely to grow larger, but that does not mean that deficits necessarily will grow larger. They may or they may not. All of the discussion above will still pertain, regardless of the absolute or relative size of government.

However, in the long run, issues such as financing Medicare, Social Security and other government programs will be particularly important and are likely to require tax increases.

The long run and the short run should be carefully distinguished. We must all realize that the long run is approached through a series of short runs. These short runs have to be adjusted more and more for sequential years as the problems of the long run are more and more closely approached.

Chapter 18

LIVING BEYOND OUR MEANS

In the US, living beyond our means has been honed to a fine art. This is true both at the national level and at the individual personal level.

The country as a whole, with its enormous import surplus, is living well beyond its means. Collectively, we are using about 106 per cent of our national income. This profligate national lifestyle is financed by borrowing from abroad and by selling American assets to foreigners. We are selling assets to and borrowing from the private foreign sector and also borrowing from foreign banks. In addition, foreign sovereign wealth funds are coming in to buy US assets.

Vast numbers of the American public are also living beyond their income. They are floating on a sea of debt. They borrow on the security of their homes, their cars, their securities, even their pensions and, of course, their credit cards. They sell their assets - their houses and their securities, hopefully appreciated in value. They draw down their accumulated savings. All this is used to finance a profligate lifestyle with a savings rate out of income of less than nothing. Americans are great spenders but lousy savers.

How is all this possible? Who is willing to pay the bill? Why are they willing to pay it?

On the country level, there are two foreign groups that make it possible for us to acquire the foreign currencies needed to finance the import surplus - the excess of imports not paid by our exports.

The private foreign sector wants to acquire American assets - stocks, bonds, real estate and US corporations - for investment and diversification purposes. Their desire to do so is strongly influenced by the size and health of the American economy and their expectations of future appreciation in the value of US assets.

The trouble is that foreigners already hold huge amounts of US assets. Some have called it quits. Enough is enough. In recent years, the acquisition of US assets by the foreign private sector has not been enough to finance the total US import surplus.

So, foreign central banks have stepped in to make up the difference, particularly Asian central banks. Their purpose is largely different. They are not trying to make a profit by acquiring US assets. They are focused on buying dollars and selling their own currencies to prevent those currencies from rising in value relative to the dollar. They do this for national competitive reasons. They want to keep their exports cheap in terms of the dollar That in turn permits rapid domestic economic growth fueled by rapid growth in exports that depends on an inexpensive domestic currency. This is particularly important for China.

On the US domestic personal level, the many financial innovations in recent decades have made it far easier for consumers to borrow. And they do so with a vengeance. Consumers borrow so much that their net savings have degenerated to the negative level. In essence then, their borrowing and sale of assets results in consumption greater than income, i.e. the current state of negative saving. All this has become particularly important in recent years due to the appreciation in the value of assets such as private homes.

This profligate lifestyle, both at the national level and at the individual private level, will get harder and harder to maintain in the future.

At the national level, foreign central banks may get tired of purchasing massive amounts of a declining asset, namely the dollar, at the existing price of the dollar. This is particularly true of China as it tries to substitute internal consumer demand based economic growth for export based economic growth more and more. Already there are voices in China worrying about what will happen to the real value of China's enormous dollar holdings as the dollar declines in value.

Foreign central banks are likely to buy dollars only at lower values of the dollar in the future. This will make the dollar cheaper for foreigners and foreign currencies more expensive for Americans. As this scenario unfolds, our exports will go up, imports down and the import surplus down. Americans will be forced to tighten their belts at least somewhat.

At the individual personal level, as the past appreciation in the value of housing increasingly has turned into depreciation, it has become more difficult to finance consumption through borrowing on the house. Consumers will have to tighten their belts a notch or two. Consumption will probably shrink somewhat as a percentage of GDP, and savings might finally emerge from the subbasement.

But it will still be true that Americans are great consumers but poor savers. So the increase in savings is likely to be disappointing. As long as there are credit cards, consumers will use them for credit, lots of credit. As long as it is possible to borrow on housing equity, they will continue to do so. The only question is, "how much?"

But we cannot expect foreigners to finance the US forever at the present pace. Nor should we have expected housing values to rise rapidly forever. Nor can we expect consumer debt ratios to rise forever. There is bound to be a reckoning. In fact, the only question, "when", has already been answered in the case of housing. We will all have to live a little less beyond our means.

Chapter 19

MORTGAGING THE FUTURE

Years ago, in another age, households actually paid for nearly all their purchases out of current income or past savings, The single large exception was the purchase of a house. Later came the purchase of an automobile.

No longer. The days of "pay as you go" have come and gone. Now, the payment for just about anything can be and is deferred to the future. Of course, eventually these bills have to be paid, but in the meantime we can enjoy today what has to be paid for tomorrow. Interest charges all add up. Indeed interest, as a per cent of the national income, has risen greatly in the last half century.

Not only interest, but also late payment fees add up. These are rapidly rising and often, with the late payment fees, come higher interest rates. For a good many, when the evil day comes when they cannot or will not pay their bills, there comes the threat of bankruptcy. And that has now been made more difficult and expensive.

Governments too can and do defer many of their obligations into the future. They borrow vast sums. This creates deficits and increases in government debt - Federal, State, Local and Public Authority.

But there is more. Many government obligations don't have to be paid right away. Obligations such as future pension payments, future Medicare payments, future Social Security payments are not fully funded, so such future obligations don't create commensurate current expense until later. This means that future governments will have to increase taxes, undertake more borrowing or decrease benefits.

In the meantime, governments too have to make interest payments on their debt. But the Federal Government has one great advantage over the private sector. It has absolutely certain eternal life. Typically it doesn't pay off its debt. It rolls it over. New debt is issued to pay off old debt. As long as the economy keeps growing, the debt ratio, i.e. the ratio of debt to GDP, doesn't necessarily go up. As long as the percentage growth of debt is no greater than the percentage growth of GDP in nominal terms, the ratio remains the same or declines. And if the debt ratio does rise, as long as it doesn't rise "too much", the Federal Government does not get into the same difficulties that face private sector debtors. Many of the States and Local Governments try to do the same as the Federal Government.

So, mortgaging the future has become common everywhere, Both the willingness and the ability of households to borrow has changed drastically in the past half century. Due to many financial innovations, it has become much easier to borrow. Credit cards, second mortgages, lines of credit on the security of the house, refinancing the house, and even negative amortization and so on either did not exist half a century ago or have become much easier since that time.

With all this easy access to credit, Americans became greater and greater consumers and worse and worse savers, The household savings rate has now fallen through the floor.

Behind the scene of this collapse of the household savings rate was a combination of substantial increase in the value of a particular asset and ever easier ways to borrow on this asset. The spectacular increase in the value of housing, 2000 - early 2006, combined with the growing simplicity of tapping housing equity, resulted in increased borrowing on the security of the house, increased spending of this new liquidity on consumption and disappearance of net household savings.

Now that housing prices have been falling, many of these borrowers, out on a thin limb, will have cause for regret as they lose their homes. They had hoped that rising housing prices would come to the rescue, but are facing falling housing prices instead.

A much larger group will not lose their homes but must come to terms with shrinking equity in their most important asset, their home. This shrinking equity is due to the more recent decline in housing prices. It has important implications.

Equity in their homes has been a highly important part of retirement finance. With shrinking home equity, millions will find their retirement hopes and plans badly askew. Essentially, more and more are consuming the home, piece by piece, during their working years, so little remains to take care of their retirement years. This can be very serious to those affected. In addition, their heirs may inherit nothing but the wind.

So, there are major problems in both the private sector and the public sector in the retirement scene. In both cases the future benefits have been mortgaged in favor of current expenditures. In the private sector, this has to do with increased borrowing on the house and the decline in saving. In the public sector, it has to do with inadequate current set asides for financing pensions, medical payment obligations, etc. in favor of current spending of the necessary funds on other projects.

PART 6: THE STATE

Chapter 20

WHO GETS THE TAX DOLLAR?

Today, there is fierce competition for the tax dollar in both Federal and State Governments. Tomorrow it will be worse.

Older government programs have a tendency to grow bigger and more expensive. As they grow, they acquire more and more powerful constituencies - beneficiaries on the on hand, suppliers on the other. The programs acquire political power. It becomes harder and harder to cut them back. Obsolete programs acquire a life of their own. Programs whose usefulness has diminished continue indefinitely.

New programs also become broader, bigger and more expensive over time. They too acquire constituencies. The bigger a program becomes, the bigger will be its constituencies, the greater its political power, the less the likelihood of taming its expansion. Social Security, Medicare, Medicaid, food stamps, all were once small programs. Now they are gigantic.

As programs expand at the Federal level they gobble up a larger and larger share of the tax dollar. Sooner or later they also gobble up borrowed dollars, increasing Federal deficits. At the State level, the programs pressure State budgets; this results in special State borrowing for specific projects to get around State constitutional balanced budget provisions. These borrowed funds free up funds for the programs in the regular State budgets. In effect, States can run at deficits.

There is not a lot of budget discipline, and long term planning is really inadequate. But this is also true in many other countries. Governments are run by politicians who have to be elected at relatively short intervals by a voting public that is unwilling to reduce the programs. Politicians respond to the public. Up to a point they must, if they expect to be reelected.

These programs are now increasingly interfering with each other in the competition for resources. At the State level, the high growth rates of expenditures on Medicaid and prisons, as well as pensions, are cutting into educational expenditures. At the college level, for example, these competing programs, as well as the growth in number of students, has caused pressure on tuition and student aid in the financing of state owned institutions. Federal funds for student assistance are also under pressure. So, in recent years, a larger and larger proportion of the financial burden has devolved on the students themselves.

In Western Europe, government medical insurance programs and pensions are eating up a large portion of government revenues, As a result, there is increasing pressure on other programs such as higher education, not to mention military expenditures.

At the State and Local level, there has also been a vast underfunding of pension contributions, The recent scandal in San Diego is a case in point. As the States, Cities and School Districts are forced to increase their pension contributions there will be even more pressure on primary and secondary education, higher education, Medicaid and prisons. The picture is not pretty.

At the Federal level, the programs that are currently in surplus, such as Social Security and Medicare A (for hospitals) will eventually move into deficits. Medicare B (for doctors) is already in substantial deficit. As these programs start taking from rather than contributing to the Federal budget, they will apply pressure to all the other government programs, and of course to the budget itself. The new drug program will undoubtedly follow the usual path of such programs, getting bigger and more expensive. That will apply still more pressure. The inevitable result will surely be growth in government expenditure in both absolute numbers and share of the national output. This could mean either unacceptable government deficits or substantial tax increases, possibly both.

Entitlements have shown the fastest growth in government expenditures and take an ever increasing portion of the Federal budget. Clearly, this cannot go on indefinitely.

In general, both the Federal Government and the State and Local Governments have exhibited a woeful tendency to ignore the future. Every year for itself and the devil take the future! What is needed is a set of social priorities and not a jerry built house that threatens to collapse. This problem is very difficult to fix in a democracy that inevitably places decisions largely in a short run context, since politicians face elections.

Western Europe has already painted itself into a corner, since very high social expenditures, growing over the years, required very high income taxes, value added taxes and business taxes to finance these expenditures; that, in turn, has had deleterious, long lasting economic consequences. We don't want to stumble into this quagmire.

So, what's wrong is clear: short run focus of government; lack of long term analysis; collision of programs for funding without any understanding of required action; expediency instead of priorities.

Chapter 21

OVERCOMMITMENT BY GOVERNMENT: "PROMISES, PROMISES"

Governments at all levels - Federal, State and Local - are overcommitted. They are not the only ones. Private sector corporations can also be overcommitted. But corporations, such as General Motors, are taking steps to reduce such excess commitments. Governments have failed to do so. On the contrary, governments are taking on even more commitments for future payments.

The fundamental problem lies in the nature of elective representatives in a democracy. Politicians must run for election, usually for two year, four year or six year terms. For reelection, they need the support of the voters. So they make promises and pass legislation to fulfill these promises: promises of future pension payments; promises of future medical payments; promises of earlier eligibility; promises of greater family coverage; promises of wider medical networks; and so on. The promises are in the present, the payments are in the future. Most current politicians won't be around when the piper has to be paid. They know that. So, from their point of view, it is an easy giveaway.

But, for public employee pensions even the most bountiful giveaways require some sort of current financial contribution. These often are in the form of deductions from the wages and salaries of public employees that are then invested in financial assets to pay for future benefits. The question is this: realistically speaking, given a technical and economic appraisal of the expected yield from these financial assets, what proportion of the promised future benefits will actually be covered when the payments are due? The answer usually is: a good deal less than the amounts actually required at that time.

With the Federal FICA taxes for Social Security and Medicare, most of the tax payments are actually used on a pay as you go basis to cover the Social Security payments to those currently eligible to receive them and the current hospitalization costs of current Medicare recipients. (Most of the current physician costs in Medicare are taken out of general Federal tax receipts.)

This is an intergenerational compact between those who are now working and those now eligible for the receipts from the programs. The former pay, the latter benefit. The social compact assumes that, later, when the current workers retire, the following generation will take up the payments. But, sooner, in the case of Medicare, and later, in the case of Social Security, the Social Security and Medicare taxes will be insufficient to pay for the actual current expenditures for the programs at such future times. So, additional sources of funds must be found. That means more taxes. Alternately, payments will have to be reduced in the future.

Another issue has to do with capital costs and maintenance costs. Government often has spent large sums on capital expenditures without adequate consideration of the decades of maintenance costs that follow. So, it becomes overcommitted, maintenance is left to slide, deterioration sets in, and even greater costs follow. Infrastructure is a good example. To be sure, the Federal

Government has tried to remedy this problem, particularly in the Pentagon, by requiring estimates of maintenance costs for capital projects. But it remains a significant issue in the States, in Public Authorities, in Local School Districts and in Local Government. Most future maintenance costs can be reasonably estimated. Such estimated annual future maintenance costs should accompany every capital expenditure plan.

These overcommitments by Government are important and will become more important. It is obvious that all the many governmental promises cannot be fulfilled in the future. There will be tax increases, of course, to give government more resources. There will be reshuffling of government expenditures. There will be more user payments to government from those who use various government services. But, when all is said and done, there will still not be enough wherewithal to allow government to fully fulfill its promises. A technical way of saying this is to say that the present dollar value of all these promises is greater than the present value of the means to pay for them.

Many, in the future, will come away disappointed. This is going to have great political implications, great taxation implications, great health care and pension implications, great implications for the aged, and much else.

Chapter 22

INFRASTRUCTURE

America's infrastructure is showing its age. Much of it is middle aged and far too much is old and even ancient, particularly in the older urban areas. Maintenance problems are growing, even as maintenance is deferred or ignored. Replacement is lagging. It is lagging because it is expensive, often very expensive. And there are many competing uses of funds - Federal, State and Local, and private sector.

As long as this increasingly creaky system keeps working, it is, "out of sight is out of mind". Don't ask, don't tell. When a crisis raises public awareness for a time, memory tends to fade quickly. When a potential crisis is widely predicted years in advance as in the case of New Orleans, very little is done to avoid it. When the crisis actually occurs, the blame game starts.

The backlog of needed expenditures is large. The American Society of Civil Engineers puts the total amount at around two per cent of our gross domestic product for each year over a five year period. It also gives a letter grade to the condition of a dozen categories of infrastructure. The overall grade was D plus in 2001 and 2003, and D in 2005.

Policies of "patch and pray" do have substantial costs. The worst example, of course, is New Orleans where inadequate, poorly constructed, poorly maintained, of insufficient height, levees failed to withstand a major hurricane. This failure exacted an immense toll in human lives, in property destruction, in financial cost, in effective abandonment of low lying parts of the city, in displacement of its inhabitants who were scattered far and wide, in public safety and indeed in the mainstays of civilization as we know it.

Then in 2007 came three events, fairly close together, that again reminded everyone of infrastructure problems. In New York, a steam pipe under a street very close to Grand Central Station exploded. In Minneapolis a major bridge over the Mississippi River collapsed sending dozens of cars tumbling down, with quite a few into the river itself. In New York storm flooding stopped most of the subway system one day, practically bringing the city to a halt.

There are many aspects of inadequacies in infrastructure: congested highways with longer commuting times; airline delays; power outages; overcrowded schools; clean drinking water problems; many transit delays and breakdowns; sewage pollution of rivers, lakes and oceans; solid waste disposal issues; water main breaks and flooding; potholes in road and street systems; dirty public parks; asbestos and lead paint problems; and so on.

Infrastructure is split between the public sector and the private sector, as well as the public regulation of the private sector.

The public sector, in turn, is divided into Federal Government responsibility, the responsibility of the States and various Public Corporations, and Local Government - counties, cities, school districts, water districts, sewage districts, park districts and many more such. Relatively few seem to have both the wherewithal and the will to contend fully with the infrastructure problems in their jurisdiction.

These jurisdictions include: the nation's roads - interstate highways, state and local roads, and city streets; Federal, state and local parks; elementary and secondary schools; bridges and tunnels; sewage disposal systems; most water distribution systems; flood control systems; a portion of the rail system; most municipal transit systems; airports and air control systems; locks on inland waterways; etc.

The private sector is also very extensive. It includes: most electric power production, transmission and distribution; the wiring in most buildings; most rail transportation; cable; the internet system; etc.

Finally, it has to be recognized that much of the private sector infrastructure is subject to regulation by government authorities. For example, production, transmission and distribution systems for electricity are largely regulated at the State level. Nuclear power facilities are particularly regulated by the Federal Government, but also by the States. Petroleum refineries are heavily regulated, indeed so heavily that no major refinery has been build from scratch in the US for years.

The major issues on infrastructure may be summarized thus: unwillingness or inability to come up with the necessary funding; inattention to growing problems; conflicts between the needs of infrastructure and environmental issues; the "not in my backyard" syndrome; disputes about the needs for upgrading and expanding infrastructure (shown sharply in school budget votes); taxation issues (who pays the costs?); etc.

Although recent disasters have served to focus public attention on infrastructure, it is not clear how long a lethargic public will continue to pay heed to infrastructure needs. But, further disasters are all but certain, so eventually more resources will have to be made available to upgrade this aging infrastructure.

PART 7: ASSETS

Chapter 23

THE WORLD OF ASSETS

The liquidification of assets is one of the profound trends of our times. Nearly every asset, short of man himself, is being turned into a form more or less readily convertible into cash through the new science of financial engineering. As a result, there has been a huge amount of liquidity sloshing around the world, affecting economies everywhere. Central banks, too, have assisted this process.

This liquidification of assets caused an increase in the valuation of such assets, a decrease in perceived risk in holding such assets, and an enormous increase in borrowing on the security of these assets.

In the period up to the summer of 2007 there had been widespread comment on the general downplaying of risk. Spreads between US Treasuries, for example, and all kinds of other obligations had narrowed. And stock markets in the third world increasingly were considered less and less risky relative to those in the West. Everywhere, risk assumed a less important position in determining asset values.

Borrowing on the security of these assets mushroomed. There was the mortgaging, the remortgaging, the second mortgage, the lines of credit of privately owned family housing. There was the borrowing in the corporate sector by firms, good, bad and indifferent. Junk bonds grew mightily. There was the borrowing by private equity, and the borrowing by hedge funds, on ever thinner equity bases, to hold larger portfolios and buy larger corporations, There was the borrowing on the security of the equities of the developing world.

And there was the result of still more financial engineering. Debt issues of all sorts were pooled with similar debt issues, then sliced into more and more "tranches" - pooled segments of different risk categories. These pooled segments were then sold to investors who wanted to hold investments with lower or higher risk. So, an investor didn't hold a mortgage; he held pieces of mortgages. In this process, the slicing of mortgages enhanced their total value. But the value of the riskiest slices was hard to determine since they traded infrequently.

Liquidity underlies not only the higher valuation of assets but also the borrowing on the security of the more highly valued assets. This liquidity then had a positive effect on consumption in the economy, fueled by the borrowing and cash outs on the now more highly valued private housing, i.e. remortgaging of housing. But it also resulted in the housing price boom in the first half decade of the new millennium, that turned into a bubble.

The combination of high liquidity, low risk evaluation, poor lending practices in the sub prime mortgage market, extreme financial engineering, inability to properly value the riskiest slices of mortgage pools, and growing doubts about the valuation of many assets led to the worldwide credit crunch of the summer of 2007. All of a sudden, investors grew dubious about the underlying value of assets and simply refused to lend on their security.

The credit crunch was, at the same time, a liquidity crunch, a credit crunch,a confidence crunch and a risk shift crunch. Confidence evaporated. Central banks around the world stepped in to provide liquidity, but the liquidity was provided to banks, whereas the real crunch was at non banks. So, the liquidity injection had an indirect effect. And, it only partially restored confidence. There was still doubt about the true value of many assets, particularly assets that were not trading.

What the central banks could not restore was the previous cavalier attitude relative to risk. The risk shift was more permanent. This meant that the now higher evaluation of risk would permanently reduce the value of many assets. It also meant that a lot of people inevitably would lose a lot of money. The previously high values of many assets would not return.

These developments in asset markets, as well as the dot com stock market bubble at the beginning of the decade, have made life extremely difficult for the Fed. The objective of the US central bank, unlike the stated objective of a number of foreign central banks, is not only the containment of inflation, but also the maintenance of the general economic health of the nation, e.g. reasonably full employment. To this has now been added a third, and controversial element, the prevention of asset bubbles. The Fed has received quite a lot of criticism because it has not prevented valuation excesses.

Alas, the Fed has only one broad principal power, rough control over the short term interest rate; it can influence, but not control, the longer term interest rates.

But, it is an old principle that one policy tool cannot control multiple objectives. To be sure, the Fed also has a series of regulatory powers and the ability to influence both the public and financial markets through its statements and speeches. Yet, even if this is taken as a second policy tool, it is not sufficient to accomplish three policy objectives.

Needed are some new policy tools, or at the very least enforcement of some older policy tools that had been left to wither, to come to grips at least partially with the subject of bubbles. For example, enforcement of some reasonable standards in the sub prime mortgage markets came only after the steep rise in foreclosures, not before.

Then there are issues related to the practices of financial engineering. As pools of mortgages are sliced into thin tranches, ranging from those with the lowest risk and the lowest interest rate, to those with the highest risk and the highest interest rate, it turns out that the higher the risk category, the less liquid the market tends to become. At times it becomes all but impossible to sell, or even value, these high risk assets, occasioning near panics or even actual panic. Several hedge funds collapsed in the summer of 2007 as a result, and a major Wall Street firm, known for its expertise in the bond markets, managed to drive two hedge funds in its specialty completely into the ground, resulting in total loss of their value, accompanied by a nosedive in its own reputation. Others followed, not only in the US but also in Europe and elsewhere.

This episode also made clear that the presence of a couple of high risk tranches was insufficient to remove all the risk from the lower risk tranches, which promptly proceeded to decline substantially in price as well in many cases.

A problem already noted above lies in the valuation of these assets at various times. Whenever market transactions are infrequent and of relatively modest size, the hedge funds holding such assets, with little to go on, have to make their own evaluations. These are likely to be on the high side to keep their investors happy and on board. Later, it can easily turn out, as in fact it did turn out in the summer of 2007, that such valuations were substantially in excess of reality.

These experiences raise some serious questions. Yes, it makes sense to slice up a mortgage pool into different risk tranches to satisfy different types of investors. But, how many slices and what kind should be permitted? The problem is that a collapse in the value of the highest risk tranches not only can spread to less risky slices, but could cause a financial panic.

This actually happened in August of 2007. Trading all but stopped in a large section of the bond market. Portfolios could not be valued properly. Investors were unable to withdraw their funds. Lenders demanded to be repaid; borrowers could not comply. The European Central Bank as well as the Fed had to step in to inject massive amounts of liquidity Such a panic is obviously exceedingly undesirable. No one knows in advance how far it can spread, what damage it can do, how long it will last. A whole new look at regulation of this sector is urgently required.

PART 8: GENERAL

Chapter 24

WASTE

Waste is a salient characteristic of the American economy. We are a rich country and can afford to be wasteful. The extent of such waste is affected by its cost relative to our income; the greater the cost, the less the waste.

We are not quite as wasteful as we used to be, primarily because the cost of wastefulness has been rising faster than our income over the years. So, the incentives have also been changing. The incentives now are to economize more on waste. But, though the incentives are more visible, they are not yet very strong. Still, everything points to a strengthening of these incentives in the future.

There are many different kinds of waste. One that has received a large amount of attention is the waste of energy. Anyone observing all the SUV's tooling around well paved city streets need look no further to understand the waste of gasoline involved.

When petroleum and gasoline prices zoomed in 2006, this waste became much more expensive; demand for SUV's plunged as a result. For Americans, gas above three dollars a gallon appears very high. But for Europeans, where the larger part of the price of gasoline and diesel resides in taxes, three dollars a gallon appears very low. They are paying five, six and seven dollars a gallon. If we are ever going to economize meaningfully on usage of gasoline, the price would probably have to at least double and probably more than double. In addition government regulations would have to encourage and require the automobile manufacturers to produce cars with more efficient engines and lower gas use per mile.

Then there is the matter of heating homes. President Carter long ago recommended a sweater in the winter inside the house. People laughed. But it was not a bad idea. Why live in overheated houses? In addition, strong incentives to install up to date heating equipment would help.

Our economy produces mountains of garbage everywhere. We are drowning in garbage. Local sites for disposal are being filled. So, this garbage must travel longer and longer distances at greater and greater expense. For example, New York's garbage mountain on Staten Island has been topped and closed. Now a large fleet of garbage trucks and rail cars wends its way out of the City for distant disposal.

A visit to any large garbage dump in the US, a visit very rarely undertaken by the average citizen, will quickly show that a great many high value items are visible. We have the best garbage in the world. In the science of garbagology, we are tops. Most local jurisdictions don't even require separation of different kinds of garbage by householders.

One problem is that people very rarely understand how the price of garbage disposal affects the pocketbook. This is true of practically all renters. It is probably also true of the vast majority of owners, who cannot or do not bother to break out the cost of garbage collection from all the other real estate taxes they pay. The cost of garbage to those who bear the burden needs to be made much clearer.

American consumers are the greatest in the world. They follow the principle of "buy, buy, buy". But this is then followed by "throw away , throw away. throw away". The US is the world's largest exporter of used clothing. It is also the world's largest exporter of high quality used clothing". There is a reason. We buy too much, use too little, dispose too quickly.

There is still another peculiar American institution, the huge restaurant meal. European visitors to the US for the first time, are always surprised at the size of the portions. Americans eat too much, gain too much weight and then require recourse to a whole industry offering weight reduction schemes. And...much of the meal that the patron is unable to consume lands in the restaurant garbage bin. Very little is fed to pigs.

Of course not everyone leaves so much on the plate. Some ask for a "doggie bag", another peculiar American institution that is not found in most other countries, presumably because their restaurant portions are much smaller so there is less waste and less need for carting the leftovers home.

It would make a lot more sense to reduce the size of these maxi portions, particularly for seniors who cannot possibly do them justice. This is beginning to be recognized in some quarters which have established a line of "senior meals" with smaller portions at somewhat smaller cost.

Then there are other, very different kinds of waste, particularly in the field of education. These are wastes of the human mind. This subject is covered elsewhere, but a few words are appropriate here. Education is an exceedingly inefficient process. Everyone talks about learning, but hardly anyone talks about forgetting. Unless the teacher builds a structure in just about any subject, much is forgotten quickly once the semester course ends. What a waste! Mathematics appears to particularly poorly taught, as evidenced by the perpetual shortage in US mathematical and engineering skills.

Then there is the lamentable lack of sufficient access to the university level (the educational level where the student must pay), due to the ever rising expense of university education combined with less than adequate financial aid. Many struggle and drop out. Others don't even start. Still others are weighed down by debt. The wasted minds are a hidden, but important result.

In summary, we need to reduce waste in all its manifestations. Only a sample has been discussed here. There is much more that has to be addressed.

Chapter 25

EXCESSES

The US economy is subject to excesses. Such excesses tend to cause trouble in the future, but also can have positive results in the short run. In recent years such excesses have had to do with asset bubbles and with national consumption.

One very important excess lies in the size of national consumption. Americans are great consumers but poor savers. Household consumption has ben running in excess of household income. Household savings are in negative territory. And, since most actual saving is done by upper income groups, a large part of the American public, namely the middle and lower income groups, have savings that are actually negative.

The government sector also has negative savings, i.e. deficits. This means that the only net domestic savings come from the business sector. But business savings are not sufficient to finance all of domestic investment. The remainder of the necessary savings - a large number - is made up by foreign savings, i.e. our huge import surplus. We are in effect importing large amounts of savings from foreign countries.

The huge excess in imports is unsustainable. And, it puts pressure on the value of the dollar. Already, in the last few years, the dollar has declined substantially relative to the Euro, the British pound and some Asian currencies. The dollar is expected to continue to decline in the next few years.

This excess in consumption is related to the ease of getting credit and, in recent years in particular up to 2006, the excess in rapidly climbing housing prices combined with the boom in the remortgaging of houses. But it is not housing alone. Ubiquitous multiple credit cards in every pocket have had major effects over the last couple of decades.

The housing price bubble was related to easy credit, including the excesses in the lending practices in the sub prime mortgage field. While it lasted, this easy credit permitted very extensive mortgage refinancing with large cash outs. These, in turn, were widely used for consumption, sustaining a high level of consumer demand in the economy. This permitted the economy to run at high levels.

But, this could not continue indefinitely. In the summer of 2007, the sub prime mortgage market imploded and the housing bubble deflated. The pied piper of excess had to be paid. Housing prices went on a downward path. Sub prime mortgages all but disappeared as lending standards were drastically tightened for those with poor credit ratings. Mortgage based assets based on sub prime mortgages collapsed. Other mortgage based assets dropped substantially in price. A severe credit crunch and confidence crisis rapidly developed. Only then did enforcement of reasonable lending standards by regulators become a pressing issue. The door was locked after the horse was stolen, perhaps in the hope that future horses would be safe from theft.

Another well known excess was the dot com stock market bubble of the late 'nineties that collapsed after the turn of the millennium. In 1929 it was said that the stock market values discounted not only the future, but the hereafter. A similar scene unfolded in the late 'nineties. When the bubble burst, many companies went into bankruptcy and whole sectors tanked. Before the bubble burst, the rise in stock market values was a real plus for investment. After it burst, the economy suffered. The Fed endured much criticism at the time as well as later for not trying to stop the mad rise in asset valuations. But a substantial rise in its major weapon, the Federal Funds rate, i.e. the shortest term interest rate, would not only have deflated asset values, but also would have had quite negative effects on the real economy, including employment. That, the Fed was not prepared to do.

The difficulties of contending with excesses in the asset markets have not been resolved. Interest rate policy alone cannot do it. Probably, there will have to be more careful, and much more timely, examination of use of the specific regulations that affect each specific and different developing asset bubble.

Chapter 26

HONEYPOT TO THE WORLD: IMMIGRATION

The fastest way for most workers in the poorer countries to improve their living standards is to move to a high income country. This is particularly true of the unskilled and semiskilled. The biggest, and in most ways the most attractive, high income country is the US.

At the other end of the skill ladder, the highly skilled find the greatest technological and business opportunities, with the highest income levels, also in the US. So, the US has become a magnet for the more venturesome of the labor force in the entire world's poorer countries. It is not the only magnet; it is just the biggest by far. Smaller magnets exist in Western Europe, Australia and elsewhere.

For the US, with its population of more than 300 million, immigration - legal and illegal - is running at somewhat less than one and a half million annually. This is a very small fraction of the total population, but it is a significant percentage, not far from one-half, of the annual increase in the US population. It helps keep the population growing, unlike Europe where nearly every country other than Turkey, and possibly Ireland, will be declining in population or has already started declining in population. This is also true of Japan which allows practically no legal immigration at all other than returning Japanese ethnics from countries like Brazil.

But US immigration policy is in a mess. The combination of wild disagreements on immigration policy and poor control of US borders has foiled all attempts to revise the immigration laws. Congress has tried to change the laws several times without success.

There are a number of interrelated issues including: border control; immigration policy; and what to do about the 12 million or so illegal immigrants (about 4 per cent of the US population) already in the country. None of these issues have been resolved. They are most unlikely to be resolved until at least 2009, if then.

In the meantime, there are disputes about the nature, length and control of fences along the Mexican border to keep out unwelcome parties. These issues have drawn ever more attention since 9/11. Border patrols have been enhanced. And there are now even vigilantes to pounce on the illegals.

At the same time, US agriculture is complaining about the dearth of unskilled farm labor to harvest perishable crops. (Some farmers are even moving their operations to Mexico where farm labor supply is ample.) Their solution to this farm labor shortage is a bracero program to permit temporary entry of agricultural workers who will all then return in due course to their countries of origin.

Immigration policy in general is torn by conflicting interests with different economic and non-economic objectives. Family reunification has been a cornerstone of US immigration policy for decades. That of course is the humane, and in many ways even moral, thing to do. The problem is that it goes on forever, it takes up a large share of legal immigration, and it fails to yield the kinds of immigrants who would be optimal for the US economy. As a practical matter, family reunification results in admission of many low skilled persons (who will never work in agriculture), often with very little knowledge of English, into an American society that requires more and more skills not available in adequate supply domestically. That is also true of most of the illegals. This results in both economic and political problems.

Business, on the other hand, is pressing for an increase in skilled immigrants. That requires some sort of a point system with points for technical degrees, English language skills, industrial experience, etc. such as systems used in Canada, Australia and a number of other countries. But in today's complex world, even that would not suffice to measure the skills of immigrants completely. Business does not want simply an "engineer", or even a "software engineer". It is looking for highly specialized people. So, business wants an expansion in the admission of those immigrants who are nominated by the employers themselves to cover their very specific requirements.

Of course the battle over skill versus family reunification could be resolved through an increase in the legal immigration quotas. Since the sum of annual legal plus illegal immigration is only about half of one per cent of the US population, a substantial expansion of legal immigration could largely resolve the issue. This is particularly true if illegal immigration is cut substantially with better border control. In some cases, as noted earlier in the case of the low skilled agricultural labor supply, failure to get enough highly skilled, specialized people into the US will result in American companies setting up programs abroad, i.e. outsourcing some of the highly skilled functions. Companies such as Microsoft have already established such centers abroad.

An even greater problem lies in the issue of that four per cent of the US population that is illegal. How can it be resolved? This has created the greatest political passion, with loud cries against "amnesty" for illegals, cries so loud that a reasonable resolution so far has not become possible. Obviously, it is not feasible to deport 12 million people, many with young children who are US citizens, others married to US citizens. And it is highly undesirable to have in our midst a large group that can be, and often is, exploited in the labor market. The greater the extent to which it is exploited, the more it will undercut the employment and wages of low skilled American workers.

In the meantime, enforcement has been stepped up. Immigration agents are raiding factories, arresting dozens and even hundreds at a time. It has to be recognized that many "undocumented" aliens are really not undocumented. But the documents are false. There are raids on their private residences to seize some illegals in the middle of the night tearing families apart and resulting in terrible publicity for Immigration Services. The theory behind all this is simple: if undocumented aliens cannot find work, they will go back to their own countries by themselves. But, the theory doesn't work. And, along with all that is involved in tougher enforcement policy, problems have been created for US citizen or permanent resident Hispanics who are fired from jobs by mistake or taken in a raid by mistake. Increasingly, such Hispanics are advised to carry ID at all times.

Some sort of legalization, with or without hope of eventual citizenship, would greatly reduce these problems. The fact of the matter is that most of the the illegals are hard working people who would make good Americans. But the illegality of their arrival is not acceptable to a substantial portion of Americans. That is where the matter stands. We should not let it stand there indefinitely. It is not good for the country.

APPENDIX

Sources

Chapters 5, 6: Data Sources described in <u>New York Times</u>, June 5, 2005, page 27

About the Author

Peter M. Gutmann is professor of Economics at Baruch College of the City University of New York.

He is the author of "Common Confusions in Macroeconomics", "Understanding Modern Macroeconomics" and "Macroeconomics in Brief". He has published in a range of economic journals including the American Economic Review, the Journal of Income Distribution, the Review of Economics and Statistics, the Financial Analysts Journal and others.

Professor Gutmann is widely known due to his pathbreaking work on the subterranean, or underground, economy which created a whole industry of articles and books by economists from all over the world on that subject.

He has a doctorate from Harvard University. His dissertation title was "Income Distribution, Asset Values and Economic Growth".

Professor Gutmann teaches macroeconomics and growth economics at Baruch College of the City University of New York.